Strategy Making in Nonprofit Organizations

Strategy Making in Nonprofit Organizations

A Model and Case Studies

Jyoti Bachani and Mary Vradelis

First published in 2012 by
Business Expert Press, LLC
222 East 46th Street, New York, NY 10017
www.businessexpertpress.com

ISBN-13: 978-1-60649-385-4 (paperback)

ISBN-13: 978-1-60649-386-1 (e-book)

DOI 10.4128/9781606493861

Business Expert Press Environmental and Social Sustainability for Business Advantage collection

Collection ISSN: Forthcoming (print)
Collection ISSN: Forthcoming (electronic)

Cover design by Jonathan Pennell
Interior design by Exeter Premedia Services Private Ltd., Chennai, India

First edition: 2012

10 9 8 7 6 5 4 3 2 1

Printed in the United States of America.

Abstract

This book offers a model for managing nonprofit organizations and illustrates it with several case studies. The strategy–structure–systems approach to managing a business enterprise is modified to include a purpose–process–people centered approach that is more relevant for nonprofit organizations. Nonprofit organizations need this modified approach because there are some fundamental differences between business and nonprofit organizations that are explained in the book. As the demand for essential social services is growing and the government budgets to provide such services are shrinking, there is a greater need for social enterprises to be managed more effectively and efficiently. Using case studies and theories of management, we offer a model that is relevant for anyone managing social enterprises. This book will answer the following questions:

- What are some different kinds of nonprofit organizations?
- What is the contribution of the nonprofit sector to the economy as a whole?
- What is similar and what is different between nonprofit and other organizations?
- How do the strategic management tools developed for businesses become useful for managing a nonprofit organization?

Keywords

social enterprise, nonprofit management, strategy, triple bottom line

Contents

Preface

Sumantra Ghoshal and Christopher Bartlett's ideas provide the foundation for this book, which started as a dialogue between the two authors: Mary Vradelis, who after 20 years of experience in the nonprofit sector was completing her second master's degree in business administration; and Jyoti Bachani, a strategy professor with several years of experience as a strategy consultant, primarily in large corporations, who was teaching the final capstone strategy class.

Mary had served many roles in the nonprofit sector, including executive director, fund-raiser, board member, volunteer, and most recently consultant. In that time, she availed herself of nonprofit trainings available on management of board, staff, and finances, including fund-raising workshops to learn to raise revenue from grants, individual donors, and special events. Mary enrolled in the MBA program after facing growing pressure to operate her nonprofits as a business. Acting more like a business meant paying attention to the bottom line, metrics, and outcomes versus inputs. Toward the end of her MBA program she started to wonder how to apply what she had learned to her nonprofit work. She was starting to feel that perhaps a lot of what she learned did not really apply to her work. She started to question it in a dialogue with her professor.

Jyoti tried to convince Mary that nonprofits are organizations that need to be managed in the same way as business organizations, since maximizing profitability or maximizing some other metrics, say social goals, requires similar management practices. Minimizing cost is good for both businesses and nonprofits. The dialogue continued past the time Mary graduated. Mary started to apply the new theories she had learned and the two of them continued to exchange books and articles to learn about their different perspectives. Finally, when these discussions were not being resolved by theory, they decided to go into the field to resolve these by empirical data gathered from several managers and leaders in nonprofit organizations.

These interviews proved to be valuable as the managers were open and forthcoming about the challenges of their work. Many of them declared the same thing as Mary, that the management training recommended for them was not serving them well. There was a need for better communication with their corporate supporters. The nonprofit leaders needed to articulate their challenges in a way that would make the business training more relevant to their nonprofits. The business leaders too could bring their expertise to bear on the management of nonprofits better if they could better understand the concerns of the nonprofit leaders. There was a need for bringing the two sides closer through a focused articulation of the differences and the identification of words that had different meanings in the two contexts. This is what we took on as the goal of our book.

In this book we blend our 40 years of combined experience with research to understand how to apply business practices in nonprofit contexts. We looked at nonprofits to understand how business management could provide answers to some of their challenges. These stories have been particularly poignant at a time when the economic crisis created a greater need for services provided by nonprofits (housing, healthcare job training, and counseling) and revenue sources from grants, donations, and earned income were shrinking. But beyond the fiscal challenges, we were moved by the stories such as that of Patrick, who realized that he might have to leave the organization he founded when the board began to apply bottom-line success metrics to a program that he considered vital to the organization's mission; or Gerard, who wondered whether his organization could continue to fund an arts program that served an important cultural community, even though it did not meet the capacity-building standards of his organization; or Jeff, who realized that his idea of an ambitious goal—one that would have been welcome in the for-profit world—was demotivating to the employees who were crucial to his youth organization's mission; or the innovative leaders who applied technology to bring medical care to thousands of patients in remote areas of Pakistan.

Both the authors are committed to making management relevant in practice. Organizations in general, and social organizations in particular, are vehicles for collective action through which human endeavors beyond the individual level are accomplished. Management of this collective effort is a challenge in the best of circumstances, and we are dedicated to finding ways in which it can be improved. Here, we take on the assumption that business and nonprofit organizations can be managed in a similar manner. There are many similarities that make this a good prescription in general, but in many cases this has not served the nonprofit organizations well. We offer some of these instances as case studies in this book. The cases have been disguised in the interest of a frank presentation of hard to discuss issues. The purpose of sharing these stories is that others can learn from their experience, and also that those in similar situations can identify how to tackle them successfully. For those unfamiliar with the inner workings of nonprofit organizations, these stories provide a flavor of what it takes to manage one. These stories, and our experience, provide the basis from which we have inductively arrived at some recommendations for the readers of this book.

We thank those who shared these stories with us. We hope that the lessons we have learned from these will be useful to them and others so that they can successfully apply management ideas to nonprofit organizations. We provide a way to build a common language to facilitate ongoing conversations between the two sectors, since we see that the same words are used in the two contexts to mean different things. Illustrating how the same ideas are applied differently is a way to create a pathway to more successful organizations. During the course of research for this book, we found the work of other authors who have also addressed this gap between for-profit and nonprofit management. We decided that these other solutions are complementary to our results and recommendations, so we have included these as further recommended readings at the end of the book.

Acknowledgments

The authors thank the leaders of nonprofit organizations for sharing their experiences with us; the School of Economics and Business Administration at St. Mary's College of California for bringing the authors together; and the reviewers and editorial and publishing teams at Business Expert Press for making this book possible. Judy Macias, John Zorn, and Steven Tulsky read early versions and gave us feedback that improved this book. Friends and family, especially Bruce Birkett and Vishnu Bachani, supported us through the challenges of writing our first book. We retain responsibility for the errors and omissions, as learning is a work in progress.

Jyoti Bachani
Mary Vradelis
San Francisco
November 2012

CHAPTER 1

A Model for Managing Nonprofits

There is tremendous unused potential in our people. Our organizations are constructed so that most of our employees are asked to use 5 to 10% of their capacity at work. It is only when these same individuals go home that they can engage the other 90 to 95%—to run their households, lead a Boy Scout troop, or build a summer home. We have to be able to recognize and employ that untapped ability that each individual brings to work every day.

—Percy Barnevik, former CEO of ABB

This book provides a set of strategic management tools with case studies to illustrate them for the leaders and managers of nonprofit organizations. It offers answers to the following questions: What are some different kinds of nonprofit organizations? What is the contribution of the nonprofit sector to the economy as a whole? What is similar and what is different between nonprofit and business organizations? How do the strategic management tools developed for businesses become useful for managing a nonprofit organization? What are the management practices prevalent in nonprofit organizations that may be better suited for their context? Can business managers learn something from nonprofit managers?

We believe that the answers to these questions will be useful to anyone who works in the nonprofit sector or wants to, and to those who partner with nonprofit organizations in various roles as stakeholders, such as employees, managers, leaders, donors, board members, advisors, and academics. This book is also likely to be useful for leaders and managers who work at the intersection of business and nonprofit organizations perhaps with public–private partnership organizations, or with a nonprofit organization that relies on donations and management representation from the business world, or with a business organization that has an interest in and operating role, even if at arm's length, with one or more nonprofit organizations.

Knowledge and expertise provide power. This book will equip readers with knowledge that they can put to use in a number of different ways, primarily for being more effective in managing in the nonprofit context. Equipped with this knowledge, leaders in nonprofit organizations can claim credit for the contributions they make to the community and society. We did not find any other article or book that provides a framework for the challenges faced by nonprofit organizations in delivering critical social services for which there is an existing large and growing demand.

The advice that nonprofit organizations ought to be managed in more business-like fashion has often led to frustration for leaders in this sector, as business practices do not address their issues. Using business practices in the social sector can be disastrous unless some basic differences between business and nonprofit organizations are understood. This book offers a framework that takes some common business practices and modifies them to add the twists necessary to make them especially relevant to nonprofit organizations. This framework will be useful to align all stakeholders toward the shared cause. Based on practical research, the ideas presented here are relevant to the real world of solving managerial problems in organizations.

The quote at the start of this chapter, from the book *The Individualized Corporation* by C. Bartlett and S. Ghoshal, reflects that when people volunteer to serve a cause they give a lot more of themselves than they do to their paid jobs. What is it about the organizational setting that, despite professionally-trained managers, leads to such suboptimal use of its human resources? Volunteering usually happens through nonprofit organizations, be it church or the local Boy Scout troop. Successful nonprofit organizations operate in a way that allows people to contribute with self-motivated dedication. The research we present here is based on several such nonprofit organizations that are managing to channel the devoted engagement of their people. There are lessons from these nonprofits that should be of interest to business leaders who wish to have organizations where employees can contribute with such enthusiasm. The individual's potential is better expressed in the activities taken on voluntarily. There is something to be learned from the volunteer sector that makes this possible.

The authors of *The Individualized Corporation*[1] propose a new manifesto for management. We use their ideas to develop a framework that is applicable in the nonprofit context. Management theory developed in business settings needs to be modified before it is applied in the nonprofit and voluntary sectors. We provide many nonprofit case studies to show how nonprofits face challenges that are different from businesses, and why there is a need to modify management theory before it is applied in nonprofit organizations. In this chapter, we introduce the basic framework that ties together all the lessons from our research into the strategic management of nonprofit organizations. This framework is derived from basic strategy tools that have been made relevant and applicable in the context of nonprofit organizations. The many case studies we use elaborate the concepts used in this framework.

Let us look at a case study that illustrates this problem of applying business practices in a nonprofit setting. Although this case is about one particular organization, similar situations occur across many other nonprofit organizations. There is an ongoing leadership and managerial conflict between the need to make the activities and programs of an organization more accountable and financially viable, versus delivering to the values and the mission of making a difference in the community.

Case Study: "Sparks Fly" at the Statewide Literacy Center

Patrick was the founder and executive director of the Statewide Literacy Center. He was in his 13th year of leading this organization that had started as his dream and had become a reality thanks to his hard work. It was incorporated in the early nineties, with a mission to inspire and celebrate a love of reading, writing, and discourse throughout his western state. By 2010, the literary center served over 30,000 people through educational and cultural programs that included: an annual lecture series; Writers in the Schools (which places professional writers in classrooms); writing camps for children and youth; The Big Read; and various workshops and events for writers and the local communities.

Patrick expressed his values through the mission of the organization. However, in the organizational setting, these same values could also create stress. One such situation arose when a new member of his management team disagreed with how values translated into action. This new staff member initiated an organizational assessment and identified a writing program for rural children that lost money every year. She recommended discontinuing the program. Patrick said, "She felt everything we do has to make excess revenue to expand and contribute to the growth of the organization. If a program isn't contributing excess revenue does it mean it doesn't advance the organization?" Although the board and staff thought the reassessment was useful, her push for business ideas didn't align with Patrick's values or what he considered to be the organization's values as well. He viewed the program to be a valuable one that reached a constituency that no one else served. This program made a real difference in the lives of some of the children who participated in it. There were no other programs for these children. Patrick felt that this one program was closest to serving the mission of the organization, and he was prepared to let it be subsidized by other programs for this one reason. She was attempting to bring business values into the nonprofit center. In Patrick's words, "this is eventually what caused sparks to fly."

This disagreement was taken to the board. It was led by two staff and one board member, and was seen by Patrick as a way to unseat him. From Patrick's perspective, this battle was a conflict between the prioritization of financial bottom line over a program's value to the community. "[Their] argument was that I was making poor business decisions for the organization."

Patrick's position was that, "we advance the organization by running programs that contribute to the quality of life in the community. The programs might not provide a financial return initially—but in the long term, could have a financial return. If communities see the value, they may be more willing to invest financially down the road." Patrick believed that the mission-driven program paid benefits that might not be monetary, but contributed to the community, leading the Statewide Literacy Center to be valued. The primary program that was in dispute was the summer camps in rural parts of the state, that were often the only cultural opportunity that those kids might have. These were valuable to the community and to the state as a whole. Patrick explained: "Grantors support us in some cases because [the programs] aren't financially viable. Programs like this also help to build relationships with grantors. The State Arts Commission's mission is to reach out to rural communities—helping them reach their mission. The National Endowment for the Arts is also interested in programs that serve rural communities nationally. Our programs serve their mission too—therefore they support it. Nobody gives you money to do what you want to do—they give money to do what they want you to do."

"This conflict made me look again at the values I was using to base my decisions on. Yes, those were my values. If someone else disagreed with me about that—then I would have to say 'bye.' If the Board had said, 'we need to water down the program', I would have felt a need to move on. In that sense it was helpful—it was reinforcing about how I was making decisions."

Fortunately for Patrick, the board, as a whole, supported his focus on the program's values and impact. They told the staff members to not bring such issues to the board anymore and to follow Patrick's leadership. At last, this year-long conflict was over, and they could go back to the business of the Statewide Literacy Center. Patrick said that her "singular idea [drive for money] had undue importance—it was a cancer ... not healthy to have a strong drive for money. Money should serve mission."

For Patrick, the story didn't end there. This was not only a question of the importance of his values aligning with the organization. It also brought into question his role as a manager and leader of a nonprofit organization. "At first, this conflict did a lot to undermine my confidence—not so much my values, but in my abilities to manage people. How did I let that happen? There are certain traits that I carry that make me conflict averse. At a certain point—I had to say—no—we aren't going there ... this isn't going to happen. I've heard your points—considered them, incorporated some of them ... and now ... this is how we need to do this. I did not do that and now I am still trying to get my feet on the ground."

After getting a personal business coach he understood how he had allowed the board and staff to get out of alignment. He had seen this conflict developing and felt he "should have said, 'Whoops, here is a place we are in conflict and out of alignment.' Right then, I should have made time to face it—ask her, 'Where are you? You are not on the same page.' My problem was that I allowed it to stay out of harmony."

A Nonprofit Management Model

Nonprofit organizations are often being asked, by their board members, consultants, and even businesses that donate to support their cause, to be more accountable, transparent, effective, and efficient. There are many business tools and management frameworks that are offered to them as a way to achieve all this. However, those who have adopted these approaches have often found that it did not lead to the results expected and, more often, was a total waste of time. They had to do it just to please the donor or board members who wanted them to adopt these business approaches that served well in the business context, but were not appropriate to the nonprofit context. Many leaders of nonprofit organizations are frustrated that the board members and donors or other stakeholders who come from the business environment do not sufficiently understand their world, yet impose these inappropriate business solutions on them.

The framework underlying the key lessons of this book is described in Figure 1.1, the nonprofit management model (NMM). This model is derived by applying the new manifesto for management proposed in the book *The Individualized Corporation* to the nonprofit context. We start with the observation that organizations, whether they are for-profit or nonprofit, are similar in some regards and different in others. While business organizations can be assumed to be mostly driven by profit-maximizing goals, and thus can be assumed to be pure economic entities, nonprofit organizations are better served by theories that recognize them as social entities with diverse goals.

A dominant management doctrine, which we will call Strategy–Structure–Systems Model (or SSS model), is based on the firm selecting a strategy that would allow it to gain sustainable competitive advantage. The strategy is implemented by setting up structures, which are an aggregation of activities and tasks. Systems facilitate and monitor how the structure delivers the strategy. Systems are designed to be enduring such that people can be replaced as parts within the system. In the SSS model, top managers set the strategy and control resource allocation,

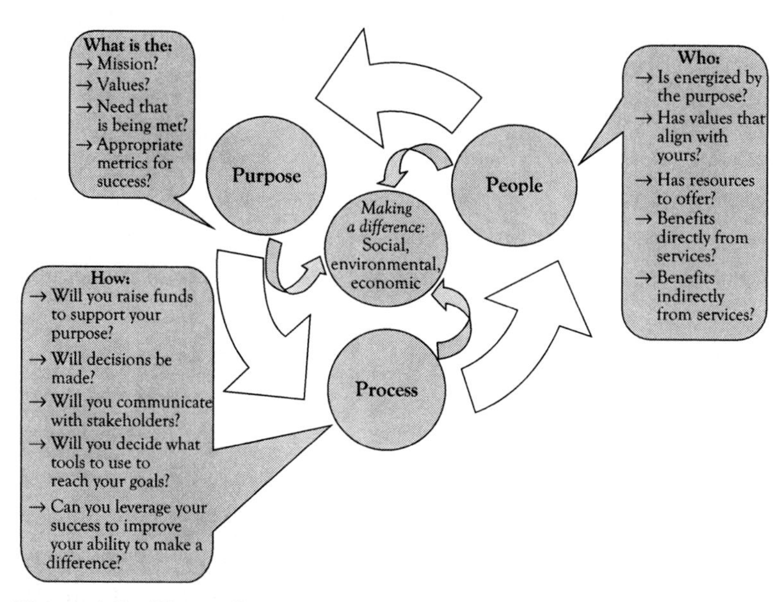

Figure 1.1. Nonprofit management model (NMM).

middle managers act as administrative controllers, and frontline managers are the operational implementers. The implementers, being replaceable parts in the system, are not expected to do much more than simply follow directions coming down the chain of command from the hierarchy. Thus, it is not surprising that intelligent, enthusiastic, frontline managers who join such organizations lose interest quickly, leading to the situation exemplified in the quote at the start of this chapter. The job becomes a means to earn a living, to pay the bills, and a mere contractual relationship.

An alternative way to conceptualize an organization is to use a Purpose-Process-People (PPP) model that focuses on it as a social entity. In addition to being an economic entity that has to manage some financial aspects, each enterprise also has multiple nonfinancial goals. An organization also has a social reason, a Purpose, for which People come to work together with agreed Processes (PPP Model) that help achieve it.

Anyone who has ever been in or around any organization would confirm that this conceptualization of an organization as both an economic and a social entity is better. The economists' assumption of profit maximizing is relevant for analytical purposes of understanding and driving the financial measures, while the social enterprise conceptualization also includes many non-financial goals. Organizations cultivate reputations for being a good place to work, or responsible community members who participate as good citizens. The people who make up organizations are not perfectly rational interchangeable parts that serve the profit-maximizing goal. People tend to find jobs with organizations that are in fields related to their interests and passions. They express themselves through their work. There are social interactions in organizations with bonds of friendships, enmity, and all manner of relationships. The employees care about the organizations they spend large parts of their waking life in. People are not robotic replaceable parts that make up an organization, but actors who participate in organizational life, bringing all the complexities of humanness into the situation. People work for many different reasons in addition to the need to make money, and take pride in making a difference through their professional achievements. Thus, organizations should also be theorized as social entities, in addition to being economic entities.

As the quote at the beginning of this chapter implies, the same person who engages with his work with a fraction of his potential can get energized to serve with enthusiasm when volunteering for a cause that he cares about. Our research with nonprofit organizations leads us to propose that a greater emphasis is needed on the PPP aspects when managing an organization. The nonprofit organizations we studied had a clear focus on their purpose, which energized the volunteers and employees they attracted; and processes by which collaborative efforts to realize the mission were carefully considered and implemented.

Throughout this book we provide several examples and case studies to show this. In the case we presented earlier the importance of purpose is borne out. Instead of focusing on the financial criteria alone, or the mission delivery alone, there was a need for a fiscally responsible process in place that would allow the people to achieve the shared purpose. In this case, Patrick asked for a management coach so that he could handle future decisions in a manner that was less stressful for the people in the organization who shared the same goal but had different ways of going about it.

Our primary contribution adds to the literature on how to adopt business practices for the management of nonprofits. The recommended reading list at the end of this book offers related ideas from the few other authors who have addressed this topic. Our recommendations are a set of modifications to common business practice such that these would be less stressful to adopt and more effective. When managers in business organizations collaborate to work with nonprofits, they would be better served if they used this framework to bridge the linguistic barriers to communication. We believe that this translation across the border of business and nonprofits will help bring businesslike efficiencies and effectiveness, with greater accountability, to the nonprofits. In sticking with language that is consistent with their cultural context, the nonprofits are less likely to alienate their leaders, employees, donors, or political patrons. The managers in our sample learned to make these modifications by learning the hard way and correcting their mistakes. We believe that others can learn from these experiences and avoid making the same mistakes by preemptively using the recommended approach to reach similar goals.

The case studies in this book are based on real organizations we studied, though the names of specific organizations and people have been changed. Occasionally, we have developed a composite case that includes common problems we saw in more than one organization. Our primary goal was to develop the most informative situations to illustrate the challenges faced by leaders of small to medium sized nonprofit organizations.

The rest of this book is organized as follows: In Chapter 2 we explain why nonprofits are important to society. By using examples, we show how nonprofits provide much needed social and human services that no one else offers. In that chapter we describe several different types of nonprofit organizations—legally, socially, culturally, and so on. We provide data on how important this sector is to the overall economic growth and prosperity of our country.

We also show what is similar and different between business and nonprofit organizations. In the next three chapters we use each P of the PPP model to provide translations of strategic management tools into the modified concepts that are better suited to the nonprofit environment. In Chapter 3, Purpose-Driven Strategy, we explain how to use the vision, mission, and metrics to set strategic direction. In Chapter 4, Processes That Engage, we describe how business hierarchy, power, or capital structure is modified to be a network of influence or fund-raising processes. In Chapter 5, People Before Systems, we show how nonprofit organizations are under unduly large influence of the founder or specific people in key positions, with their values having a huge impact on the organization, much more so than in comparable business situations where systems make people more dispensable or replaceable. In the final chapter the key tools are summarized for easy reference, and the limitations for this research are provided so that managers can know the boundaries within which these lessons are most relevant. The majority of our cases are small to medium sized nonprofit organizations, so the lessons from the book may be more relevant to similar sized organizations. In our experience, we found that larger nonprofit organizations tended to be run more like business organizations.

CHAPTER 2

The Role of Nonprofits in Society

Case Study: Telemedicine for Rural Healthcare

According to the World Health Organization (WHO), in 2010, Pakistan had 160 million people, 70% of whom, primarily the rural population, had never seen a doctor in their lifetimes. One in 10 children there died by the age of five.[1] Eighty percent of deaths in the country were caused by preventable diseases. This dismal condition was not because there were too few doctors or an epidemic of incurable diseases. Pakistan had over 100,000 doctors, approximately one for every 2,000 people, and 1,000 government hospitals. However, the doctors tended to be concentrated in the metropolitan areas where patients could afford their services, while the predominantly rural population suffered because of poverty and distance.

The medical solutions and innovations in disease control for most of the diseases they suffered from had been developed decades ago, but a sustainable way for these to reach the rural populations was yet to be found. Remote clinics or travelling doctors to bridge the distance were so costly that governments and aid organizations were only able to treat a very limited number. Businesses in medical trade were not likely to bring existing solutions to the people who needed them desperately, because there was no money to be made. These societal problems needed to be addressed. Such problems exist in all parts of the world. Governments, nonprofit organizations, or voluntary groups tackle these ills in society.

In Pakistan, the United States Agency for International Development (USAID) and the Higher Education Commission of Pakistan (HEC) had started a Tele-Healthcare program that treated 250 patients a day with

50 trained Lady Health Workers in rural Mardan, in the North-West Frontier Province. Similar programs existed in India, Mozambique, Uganda, and other parts of the world. Nonprofit organizations had introduced telemedicine programs that deployed recent innovations in information technologies and mobile telephony, and offered affordable ways to connect patients in remote rural areas, even in the absence of roads or rails, with doctors in urban areas. The primary contact for the patients was their familiar local midwife or healthcare worker, who was trained remotely to offer basic healthcare, and to collect and transmit patient data. Doctors sent the treatment instructions back to the telemedicine operator who in turn passed the directions back to the local community-based healthcare worker's mobile device so that she could ultimately treat the patient. Medical records collected during patient consultations by the field worker could be statistically collated and analyzed to better understand the varying healthcare needs of the different regions of a country. Governments could use this data to make evidence-based decisions for setting policy priorities and budgeting limited funds according to the greatest and most urgent needs.[2]

Nonprofits Serve Crucial Social Needs

The case above illustrates the important role that nonprofit organizations play in society. Nonprofits serve critical needs of local and global communities. Being called "Not-for-profit" reflects the bias in the capitalistic society toward profit-making organizations. However, many crucial societal needs are not likely to be served by profit-making enterprises. A nonprofit's bottom line can be seen as its desire to make an impact in at least one of three realms: social, environmental, and/or economic. In the telemedicine case, the objective of the program was to deliver affordable healthcare to the rural poor.

Lester Salamon, in *America's Nonprofit Sector: A Primer*,[3] identifies five rationales to understand the diverse contributions that nonprofits make: Modernization—providing community support that earlier traditional societies would have provided through families and tribes; Market Failure—public and goods that for-profits don't have the incentive to sell or protect; Trust—consumers can rely on the fact that the service/product supplier's motive isn't profit; Pluralism/Freedom—nonprofits can provide a flexibility and freedom of diverse expression; and Solidarity—nonprofits offer a forum for voluntary associations, with a capacity for joint action. Thirty years ago there was little hard research on the sector.[4] Today there is more widespread recognition that there are several societal needs where there are no profits to be made in fulfilling them—and yet these needs must be fulfilled.

Different Types of Nonprofit Organizations

For the purpose of this book, we chose to use the broadest possible definition of a nonprofit organization. In this book, the term *nonprofit* is a catch-all category that is inclusive of all forms of organizations as long as they are not a business operated for profit. Any organization that served the community was included, be it officially defined as a nonprofit, government, quasi-government, or social enterprise. A majority of such organizations are in the role of providing community services and do so without a profit motive.

There is a common misperception that nonprofit service organizations cater to only low-income and under-represented/underserved members of society. A number of them do indeed provide social services or community support activities that are essential to people's lives—healthcare for the uninsured, care for the elderly, temporary housing for the runaway youth, job-training and job-seeking support for the unemployed poor, and so on, do target disadvantaged segments. However, many nonprofits also provide noncritical services and activities that enrich the lives of people of all income levels through programs such as private schools and universities; childcare and adult recreation programs; fine arts performances and exhibits churches; and professional associations. In our research, we focused on organizations that serve all manner of societal needs, as long as profit was not a central motivator. The primary distinction was from organizations that are driven primarily by profit.

In focusing specifically on nonprofits, our working definition of nonprofits comes from *How to Form a Nonprofit Corporation in California* (2009). Mancuso defines a nonprofit as: A legal structure authorized by state law allowing people to come together to either benefit members of an organization (a club, or mutual benefit society) or for some public purpose (such as a hospital, environmental organization, or literary society). This broad definition actually encompasses 27 different classifications of nonprofits, which are exempt from taxes according to the US Internal Revenue Service (IRS). The most recognized class of nonprofit is the 501(c)(3) in which the organization's donors receive tax credits for their donations. These include a broad range of groups, including religious organizations, charitable service organizations, scientific research organizations, literary groups, and educational institutions.

In addition to these organizations there are several different classifications that are tax-exempt but their donors do not receive tax credits. These may vary by the state. For example, the legal structure in California allows people to come together to benefit members of an organization (a club, or mutual benefit society) or for some public purpose such as a hospital, environmental organization, or literary society. The California mutual benefit organizations' members do not receive tax credit, and include trade associations, chambers of commerce, credit unions, political education, and so on (including organizations such as the National Dental Association and the Institute of Civil Engineers). Lester Salamon divides nonprofits by their contributions to society: service provision; advocacy and problem identification; expressive function; social capital; and value guardian.[5]

In the book *The Practice of Adaptive Leadership*, Heifetz divides organizations into three main sectors. These are: mission-driven nonprofits, the public sector that is "insulated from the pressure to adapt from market-place competition," and the profit-driven private sector that operates in a highly competitive environment.[6] The organizations that we focused on reflect a wide variety of tax-exempt organizations, including a statewide literary organization; a local youth development program; a regional arts education organization; two government departments—one focusing on law enforcement and the other on arts; and healthcare organizations.

The definitions and categories of nonprofits continue to evolve as their impact in society grows and the boundaries between sectors blur. Seven states in the United States have now authorized B-Corps (benefit corporations), which resemble traditional for-profit corporations, with an added focus on positively impacting their communities (socially and environmentally). These organizations have expanded their responsibility to shareholders to include social and environmental impacts in addition to the usual fiduciary responsibilities. In the past 10 years there has also been more focus on social enterprises, organizations that are applying business or market-based strategies for a social cause.

The Nonprofit Sector in the Economy

In the United States, over the past 30 years, the nonprofit sector has shown unprecedented growth and an increasing impact on the economy. According to "Quiet Crisis,"[7] the nonprofit sector contributes more than $322 billion yearly in wages and its workforce outnumbers the combined workforces of the utility, wholesale trade, and construction industries. With 9.4 million employees and 4.7 million full-time volunteers, the nonprofit workforce consists of more than 14 million people, which totals roughly 11% of the American workforce.[8] In addition, the US Bureau of Labor Statistics reports more than 64 million Americans volunteered time to an organization in the last year.[9] In 2008, nonprofit organizations were estimated to represent 5% of the United States GDP. According to 2007 studies, the nonprofit sector had total revenues of $1.963 trillion. If the sector were a country it would exceed the revenues of most countries in the world including Australia, Brazil, Canada, India, and Russia,[10] making it the seventh largest economy in the world.

According to the IRS the number of registered nonprofits nearly doubled in the past 10 years and grew 2.5 times since the 1980s (Table 2.1). In April 2009, the IRS recognized over 1.5 million nonprofits. This was a 30% increase compared to May 2000, and a 63% increase since August 1995. In 2006, California alone had 102,677 nonprofit organizations.

The National Center for Charitable Statistics has specific details of this extraordinary growth in the nonprofit sector. The largest single nonprofit category, 501(c)(3) public charities, included over 950,000 organizations and accounted for three-fourths of nonprofit revenue and six-tenths of nonprofit assets. According to the Urban Institute's National Center for Charitable Statistics, Core Files (Public Charities, 2008), health and human services accounted for over 150,000 of those nonprofits, followed by

Table 2.1. Number of Nonprofit Organizations Registered by Decade

IRS Ruling Date	Number of Registered Organizations	
Pre-1950s	162,370	10.30%
1950s	67,403	4.30%
1960s	137,711	8.70%
1970s	168,144	10.70%
1980s	167,086	10.60%
1990s	256,817	16.30%
2000s	406,726	25.80%
Unknown	209,548	13.30%
Total	1,575,805	100.00%

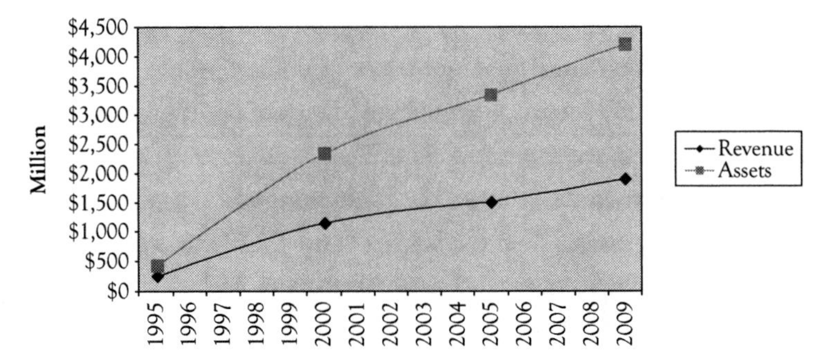

Figure 2.1. Growth of the nonprofit sector by revenue and assets.

education (64,326), public and social benefit (44,023), and arts and culture (38,759). Both the revenue and the assets of these nonprofit organizations grew significantly in the 14-year period between 1995 and 2009 (Figure 2.1). This growing and important sector encompasses a wide variety of organizations.

A Growing Demand for Social Services

Nonprofits have a significant impact on the US economy and face the same challenges that a weak economy imposes on all that participate in it. The rapid expansion in the nonprofit sector has occurred partly due to the increasing demand for their services, especially in the aftermath of the 2008 global economic downturn. The environment is also one of increased competition to gain donors, foundation grants, volunteers, and board members, as well as government contracts. The evaporation of wealth has reduced donations from individuals as well as private foundations. In addition, state and local governments have slashed their contracts for social services. "Since the vast majority of nonprofits are small to midsize organizations—roughly 94% have an annual budget of under $1 million—any reduction in funding is felt severely."[11] This economic challenge has forced nonprofits to shift their focus to fund-raising and away from development of programs, compromising the impact they could have had. Some of the nonprofit leaders we spoke with lamented the reality that they had to devote 50% of their time to fund-raising efforts even though they would have preferred to be devoting all their time to their cause.

Nonprofits are facing increased demand for their services. According to one survey by the Nonprofit Finance Fund, over 85% of nonprofits reported an overall rise in demand, with four consecutive years of growth.[12] In most cases the demand for these services far outstrips the supply. In the 2012 study, 57% of agencies reported that they were unable to meet demand.[13] There are waiting lists and selection criteria to limit and select which clients they can serve with their limited resources. Nonprofits often have to turn people away for lack of resources to meet all the need.

In contrast, the for-profit businesses usually have substantial advertising budgets and promotional programs to generate demand and awareness for their products and services. A number of the products and services offered by business organizations are not in the same category of critical or essential services as those provided by community organizations. The challenge of meeting a high level of existing demand with limited, or decreasing, resources is common in the nonprofit sector.

Nonprofit and for-profit leaders may be better able to address unmet societal needs by working together. The greater focus on corporate social responsibility is an indicator that this is being recognized. The social enterprise movement signals that even nonprofits providing social goods and services need to be acting like entrepreneurial organizations. Such collaborations are likely to rise. To make these productive, it is good to understand the core differences between nonprofit and for-profit organizations. The leaders and managers of business and nonprofit organizations will be able to cooperate and go between the two worlds if they appreciate the similarities and differences between nonprofit and for-profit organizations.

Business and Nonprofit Organizations

Many business leaders assume basic similarities between their organizations and social enterprises. They fail to recognize some of the challenges that nonprofits face. After all, a majority of the organizational issues are identical whichever sector the organizations belong to. All organizations are formed with the intent to enable collective action. All organizations need to hire and train people, have specific roles for individuals, and have an organizational culture and structure that enable the coordination of these individual actions into a consistent collective outcome. All organizations need some resources devoted to achieving their aims, such as physical space, financing for capital and operating expenses, equipment, human resources, and even some intangible resources such as reputation, goodwill, and know-how.

Capabilities to produce, market, and deliver their goods and services effectively are also necessary for all organizations, regardless of whether their final goal is to make a profit from these operations or not. As summarized by Silverthorne, "Both types of organizations can grow, transform, merge, or die. Success is not guaranteed for either type of organization, but requires sustained work. In both cases, cash is king. In both settings, good management and leadership really matter. Delivery of service, motivating and inspiring staff, and conceiving of new directions for growth are all vitally important. Planning, budgeting, and measurement systems are vital in both settings. Both types of organizations face the challenges of integrating subject matter specialists into a generalist framework. Both organizations add value to society. They just do it in different ways."[14]

Thus, it is not a surprise that business leaders expect nonprofits to act in the same way as their business organizations. When the business leaders donate to nonprofits or serve as board members for nonprofit organizations, they tend to hold them to the same standards of accountability that they are used to in their business organizations. It is reasonable to demand that nonprofit organizations deploy their resources judiciously in order to achieve their organizational goals, although the means need not be the same due to the fundamental differences between the two types of organizations.

The Differences Between Business and Nonprofit Organizations

There are a few key differences between business and nonprofits that impact how these organizations need to be managed. A number of these are not understood even by those who have worked on both sides of business and nonprofit enterprises. Let us consider these differences, so that nonprofit and for-profit leaders can improve their ability to cooperate.

Even nonprofits that appear to function as an incorporated business are not held to the same standard of strictly quantified financial measures—be it profits, or earnings per share, or return on sales—in the way that businesses are. They deliver to their own set of financial goals, such as the same services for a lower cost or more efficient use of other assets. Indeed, most nonprofits have adopted measures that make them accountable to their donors, for example by declaring the percentage of every dollar that goes to the cause versus to overhead and other administrative expenses.

As we have described before, nonprofits often serve unmet societal needs. In most cases, the demand for these services far outstrips the supply. There are waiting lists and selection criteria to limit and select the clients that they can serve with their limited resources. They often have to turn people away for lack of resources to meet all the demand there is. In sharp contrast, for-profit businesses usually have substantial advertising budgets and promotional programs to generate demand and awareness for their products and services, not all of which are critical or essential in the same way as the services provided by community organizations.

The challenges of meeting a high level of existing demand with limited resources are unique to the nonprofit sector, and seldom a problem in the business world.

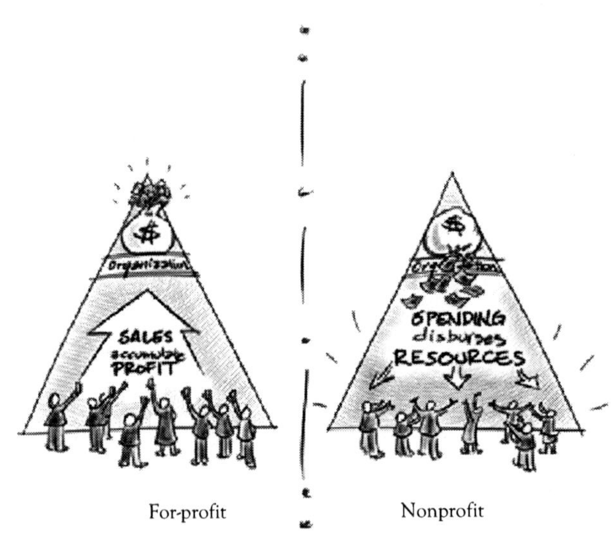

Figure 2.2. Flow of financial resources.[15]

Another way that nonprofits are different is in how the financial resources flow (Figure 2.2). Business enterprises make money by sale of products and services. In this case, the money flows from the many consumers toward the few who control the organization. For nonprofits, there is a reverse flow of financial resources, from the few who finance the organization to the many it serves. Many nonprofits do not generate revenue through sales of products or services, and in fact products and services are distributed to those who need them the most at cost, or below market price. In the *Stanford Social Innovation Review*,[16] Judy Vredenburgh cautioned, "Every time we in nonprofit satisfy customers, we drain resources, and every time for-profits satisfy a customer, they get resources back. That sounds very simple, but it has huge implications, and I don't think the for-profit people get that."

Many nonprofit leaders believe that their organizations cannot and should not be run like a business, despite this strain on services, and apparent need for operating efficiencies. They find the pressures toward a more quantitative finance-driven approach to managing their organizations to be frustrating, and a symptom of all that is wrong with business organizations. They argue that the reason for the nonprofits to exist in the first place is that no business will ever provide the products and services that are needed, as these are social goods that can only be provided on a cost-plus basis. They also argue that the social goals that they meet cannot be quantified in the same way as the bottom line of a business.

This subset of leaders of nonprofits only adopts business practices under duress, in order to please their donors and to appease the business representatives serving on their boards. They do not see much practical use for these business practices. They consider it a necessary evil or, more honestly, a total waste of time and resources. One nonprofit leader said, "Other leadership programs [that have a for-profit perspective] didn't work. They focused on how to be a better manager, supervisor, work with a board but it didn't take it to another level." They believed that the training money would be better spent in serving their cause, since the management training is not relevant to their world.

In the *Chronicle of Philanthropy* (*Donors Demand for Results Can Challenge Nonprofit Groups,* 4/21/2011),[17] Stuart Davidson, a managing partner of Labrador Ventures, said that entrepreneurial donors sometimes look at nonprofits with the "exclusively private-sector perspective" which doesn't include the complex realities and challenges of a nonprofit. In the same article Pierre Omidyar (philanthropist and eBay founder) predicted that the next generation of philanthropists will increasingly look to for-profit models for the solutions to unmet social needs. In fact, a New York Times article *Philanthropists Start Requiring Management Courses to Keep Nonprofits Productive* (7/29/11) described several large philanthropists including Omidyar and Peter B. Lewis, whose charities require management training and business development support as a part of their charitable grants. Mr. Lewis said he had intended the Management Center to provide human resource and consulting assistance to newly developed progressive groups he was underwriting at the time. "They weren't so interested, so I finally had to say, 'I won't give you any more money until you learn this stuff.'"

Good business practices can positively impact a nonprofit organization's ability to meet its mission, provided everyone involved is able to understand the differences between nonprofits and for-profits. In addition, we recommend creating a common understanding of these differences for leaders from business and nonprofits so they can work together to better meet the social, economic, and environmental goals that are critical for a sustainable world. Through our research, we identified some of the differing perspectives between nonprofits and for-profits. Below is a table (Table 2.2) that summarizes these differences:

Table 2.2. Differences Between For-profits and Nonprofits

	For-profits	Nonprofits
Mission/ organization's reason for existence	To provide the services/ goods for which communities will pay	To serve some unmet needs in the community, often something the founders are passionate about
Bottom line	Financial	Financial is secondary—only needed to serve mission
Employee motivation	Money and career growth	Cause is primary and working environment is very important
Flow of resources	Money flows from many to few	Money flows from few to many
Leadership communications and decision power	Executive and hierarchical—has power of position and rewards	Legislative—depends on consensus building to incorporate employees, donors, and followers' interests and goals
Governance	Board controlled by representatives of the people who profit from it	Board comprised of representatives of the public to ensure adequate use of the resources for the population served and the interests of the citizens overall
Resources available	Organizations have money to invest in professional development and operations	Organizations often operate with scarcity mentality
Success metrics	Mostly financial	Impacts on community, which can sometimes be difficult to measure
Fund-raising	Based on financial success or potential	Tailored to donors interests
Market share—competition vs. cooperation	Identifying the total number of potential customers and designing strategies to increase a company's percentage of the total	Understanding the need of clients and where other service providers might be leaving some people under-served—in order to make sure that gap is filled
Scalability	Replication to increase profits	Program expansion weighed against local stakeholder interests

The following chapters describe the obstacles that nonprofits have encountered when applying business principles and elaborate the PPP management strategies that they've used to work better with their for-profit supporters.

CHAPTER 3

Purpose-Driven Strategy

The raison d'être for a nonprofit is its purpose. Nonprofits exist to make a difference, whether through the services they provide for their constituents or by impacting some social, environmental, or economic justice issue that is their purpose and forms their "bottom line." The Nonprofit Management Model (Figure 3.1) offers a set of questions that can be used to engage the management and staff in a dialogue about the purpose of their organization. Answering these questions brings in the discipline and wisdom of business practices with sensitivity towards the issues pertinent to nonprofit organizations.

The Importance of Purpose

Many business and nonprofit leaders see defining the purpose of their organization as the core of their work. They may describe it as a mission

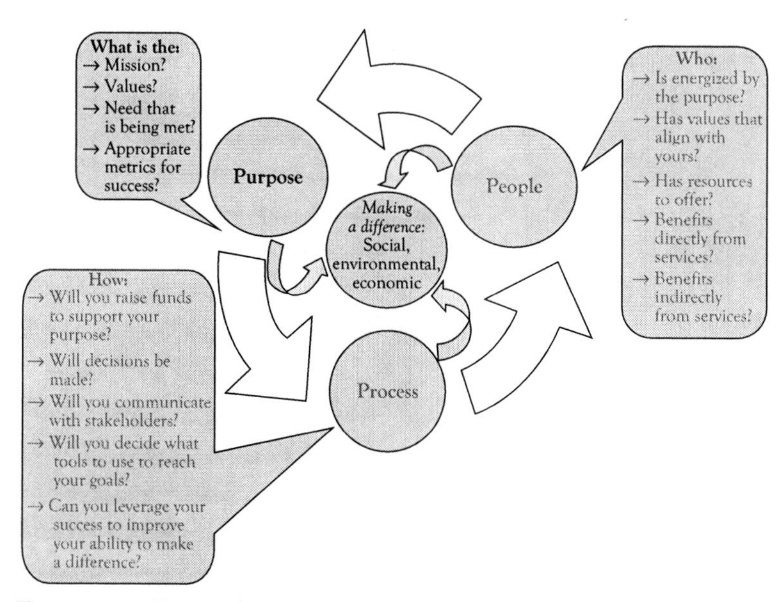

Figure 3.1. Nonprofit management model: Purpose.

or vision statement. Mission statements are important enough that they routinely appear on company websites and annual reports. The mission statement guides the daily decisions and distinguishes how the organization is seen by its clients or stakeholders.

The nonprofits we studied had leaders who had a clear focus on the organization's purpose. The purpose served four main functions: it energized the stakeholders, including staff, volunteers, and donors; it supported collaborative efforts by keeping the mission in the forefront of each partner's mind; it gave a way to find new directions, especially when an organization was buffeted by different stakeholder interests; and lastly, it provided a vision of success, around which monitoring metrics could be developed.

Case Study: From Market Share to Mission

Creating Learning was a small arts education nonprofit that placed professional artists into elementary and middle schools to enhance learning by leading students in a variety of hands-on art experiences. With a total annual budget of $300,000, it operated with minimal staff. The dedicated Executive Director (E.D.), Laura, was the only full-time employee. She was doing the program and fund-raising management as well as fulfilling leadership, financial management, and administrative duties. Laura was assisted by a part-time program coordinator and a contractor who helped with grant writing.

Despite the limited staff hours, the program served several thousand students each year by bringing artists into several urban school districts. For one mid-sized city that had an enrollment of 60,000 in their school district, they served approximately 10% of the students. In its 27th year, the organization had survived significant spikes and plummets in funding—that had left it running on a deficit in the previous year. In fact, the board feared it would have to close Creating Learning's doors. The organization relied on donations (from individuals, grants, and special events) for 55% of its budget. Earned income (program service fees from schools) only comprised 45% of its entire income. By reducing staff and administrative costs, the board and the E.D. were able to reduce the operating deficit and restore stability to the organization. This enabled the organization to return to its basic service numbers of approximately 6,500 students per year.

Anticipating a brighter future, Laura and the board developed an ambitious one-year plan to increase the number of students served by 18%. They initially designed this plan with the assumption that they could meet the goal of expansion without any additional costs. The E.D. recognized that in order to meet this ambitious goal she needed additional staff to increase fundraising from foundations and individual donors. She developed a plan to present to her board in order to get approval for funding to hire additional staff.

In evaluating the proposal, the Board President Alan drew on his business experience and background to ask, "What is your market share?" Laura was baffled. Initially, she didn't know what "market share" meant. As a small nonprofit, she hadn't considered the size of the market, or how it might affect the expansion. She only knew that, in order to meet the goal of serving additional students, she needed more fund-raising capacity. The fees paid by schools generated less than half of the cost of providing the program, so revenue had to be generated through donations and foundation grants. Alan, on the other hand, was using his business principles of revenue and costs in order to understand if additional staff would be a good investment for the organization's long-term health. He had never worked with such limited resources, where surveying to assess market share would have been prohibitive with their limited current staff capacity.

Does Growth Fit the Mission?

How would the PPP approach have helped Alan and Laura or others facing a similar situation? The model has a set of questions about the purpose of the enterprise. They could have asked themselves some questions on how best to manifest the purpose: How does expansion serve their mission? What is success in fulfilling their purpose and what are the appropriate metrics to measure success? Specifically, they could have examined the purpose of the expansion to see if their goal was to serve all the students in the county or was it to reach an economy of scale so that fund-raising and expenses would be more sustainable? Were there other organizations in the area serving the same need? Since other organizations weren't competing to meet the same mission, perhaps explicit collaboration with other organizations would have increased the ability to reach the goal of bringing arts education to more students. Clarity of purpose would have been useful to create and choose amongst the options on how best to increase the number of students. Asking these questions would have also been useful in identifying and creating the appropriate measures of success to evaluate their goals. Thus, any additional expense incurred would have been transparently tied to delivering the social bottom line, and the organization would have been operated in a fiscally responsible manner to maintain its long-term health.

Metrics to Measure Purpose

For any organization, clarity of mission is critical to its success. When the mission does not mean financial success, finding the right metric to assess and measure it can be a challenge. It is similar to finding a business model for its operations but without a focus on financial bottomline only. In fact, in his book *Integrating Mission and Strategy for Nonprofit Organizations* Jim Phills, Jr. cautions that a nonprofit's mission, "cannot for example, explain, predict or ensure an organization's financial viability."[1] In the case of Statewide Literacy Center, presented in Chapter 1, the importance of purpose is central to Patrick's leadership of the organization. Instead of focusing on the financial criteria or the mission delivery alone, Patrick had to develop a fiscally responsible process that would allow his board and staff to achieve the shared purpose. For a program that wasn't generating enough revenue to support itself, Patrick focused on the ways that it contributed to the quality of life in a community: how it provided services to a community that was not reached by other programs in the state. He sought funding partners that would invest in the program. He used the values of the organization and its purpose to guide his revenue allocation decisions.

The book *Nonprofit Sustainability*[2] offers a matrix map that helps organizations understand where a program is within an organization's desired community impact, as well as its profitability. Balanced together, an organization can focus its attention on programs that have high impact and high profitability, as well as on its portfolio of how many programs with high impact and low profitability it can afford to keep. Or, how many programs with low impact and high profitability it must maintain to keep the organization sustainable.

Case Study: Regional Arts Funding Organization

Gerard was the director of the Regional Arts Funding Organization (RAFO). Its mission was to allocate funds to various arts organizations within the region. Its purpose was to fund the arts so the region would be more vibrant and attractive to tourists. The funds that RAFO allocated were generated by a service fee collected from all tourists who stayed in the region. RAFO had a budget of $12 million in grants funds and funded almost 200 arts organizations every year. It had been doing so for a long time. The grants were given primarily to nonprofit arts organizations for the purpose of public programming. The funds were granted on an annual basis. Gerard's job involved reviewing proposals from various organizations and recommending or rejecting funding requests. Before recommendations were final, he talked to his advisory board and met with representatives of arts organizations, as well as with other funders.

One organization, Ethnic Arts Legacy, had been funded by RAFO for many years. Gerard was confronted by the difficult decision of whether or not to continue its funding. While it met RAFO's basic eligibility criteria, Gerard knew that Ethnic Arts Legacy had been losing its vitality for years. It was no longer as accessible to community members as it used to be and it had trouble retaining staff to run it effectively. In good conscience, Gerard questioned whether RAFO's funding should be used to support an organization that was no longer making a solid contribution to RAFO's mission of making the city more vibrant with community involvement in the arts. However, if Gerard withdrew the funding for the organization, it would have hastened the demise of this once vibrant organization that had an important place in the hearts and minds of community members.

The Funding Process and Criteria

RAFO did not have explicitly stated values as an organization but its focus was to build and sustain the arts ecosystem by promoting stability. The organizations funded by RAFO had to meet certain criteria. The groups were not always the most exciting or interesting groups if they were to be judged by audience or budget size. Gerard felt that RAFO and some of the groups it funded were in a somewhat co-dependent relationship since RAFO's funding essentially kept those organizations alive—supporting stability, sometimes at the cost of vitality. At the same time, the size of the fund was dependent on the amount contributed by tourist dollars, which presumably was increased by a diverse array of attractive performances. These were difficult choices, complicated further by regional politics.

The annual funding review process was elaborate. It included information sessions and opportunities for arts organizations to get feedback and improve their proposals. The RAFO staff reviewed and ranked all the applications and made funding recommendations. The process took several months. The review included site visits to better understand the make-up of the arts organization's administrative structure, programs, audience, and public profile: the draw for tourists (and their tourist dollars). Recommendations were presented to the advisory board, which was made up of community members who were appointed by the regional manager—who was also a political appointee. The advisory board made the final decisions. Depending on the size of the organization, and their scale, RAFO typically funded a modest percentage of the organizations' budgets. For some organizations, RAFO was their last hope for grant funding that supported their basic operating expenses.

After decisions were made, Gerard knew that RAFO's decisions could be questioned by the regional manager, as well as by the public at open community meetings and hearings. Applicants who didn't like the results could also appeal to the advisory board.

The potential for public outcry and the resulting challenges from the regional manager led Gerard to question if he could cut Ethnic Arts Legacy funding, even if it didn't add much to the vitality of the region. It was a long-standing organization with diminished programs and high staff turn-over. It hadn't done any systematic fund-raising for several years. RAFO's funding process could affect Ethnic Arts Legacy's vitality, yet the review process did not have any written measures to evaluate the vitality or diversity that it brought to the region. So, despite the concerns,

RAFO did not have a way to cut funding for Ethnic Arts Legacy, since it met the basic criteria by which applicants were assessed.

Gerard knew that, with its long history, if the funding for the Ethnic Arts Legacy was cut there would likely be a community uproar. He knew it was an organization that would be hard to replace. With its diminished resources, one RAFO staffer described it as putting your "grandmother on the ice flow." Yet, by continuing to fund it even in the face of its diminished capacity, RAFO's funds were potentially not being put to the best use.

Ethnic Arts Legacy did worthwhile things, and if RAFO followed the letter of the law, it should be funded. However, Gerard knew that it contributed little to the mission that was fed by the fees generated by tourist dollars—which supported arts organizations throughout the region. This dilemma left Gerard and RAFO looking for another way to define its criteria to really address its core mission of using the tourist fees collected to bring more vitality to the area. Or to expand the mission, recognizing that there was also value in stabilizing organizations that, although less attractive to tourists, also offered critical cultural knowledge to the community. In the midst of all of this, it had to pacify the many political voices in the community.

Do the Metrics Match the Purpose?

In the above case RAFO had clear eligibility criteria and process in place to determine if an organization should receive funding. Eligibility criteria focused on the amount of programming, the size of their budget, the audience statistics, etc. However, the staff also knew there were other tacit factors that influenced their decision—for example, could the service it provided the community or the culture it represented be replaced by another organization? In this case, they were clear on their mission and the goal of increasing the social and economic outcomes for their regional government. They could improve the metrics by making the tacit factors explicit to better match their goals. What support did it have in the community? How attractive was it to tourists whose fees added to RAFO's coffers and ability to fund newer organizations? Although making the tacit factors explicit and measurable is difficult, it is worth doing.

Clear metrics are critical for an organization such as RAFO to ensure it is meeting its mission.

When nonprofits question if they are making a difference, or what are the best processes to institute for their program, they will benefit from checking the practices for being in alignment with their purpose. The measurable goals also include cash and financial targets as long as it is recognized that these are not the primary measures of success but enable other goals for nonprofits. A clearly articulated purpose guides everyone within and outside the organization on a day-to-day basis as they make their operational decisions. Poorly articulated purpose can dilute the effectiveness and make it a challenge to manage the organization—as was seen in the case of RAFO and Ethnic Arts Legacy and with Creating Learning. A clear purpose, linked with appropriate success measures, can help keep the organization on track. When the metrics for a nonprofit's purpose are hard to quantify as an output, even approximate or subjective measures help an organization continue to improve performance.

CHAPTER 4

Processes that Engage Structures

Good processes are key to successful nonprofit management. A manager with experience in running successful business organizations may recommend structural tools—such as an organizational chart, assembly line, management flow of information, or others—in order to make a nonprofit organization more effective. In doing so, he might find that the tasks and activities of a nonprofit organization may not lend themselves to the same structural efficiencies as a business. Many organizations we researched showed us how often these systems went awry in a nonprofit setting. Instead, leaders were able to achieve effectiveness and efficiency by focusing on processes that align the organizational tasks and activities

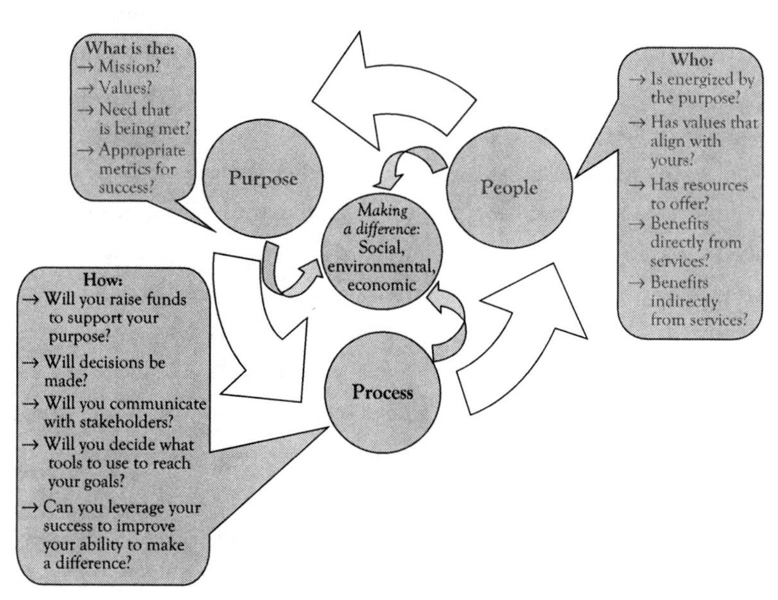

Figure 4.1. Nonprofit management model: process.

such that people were enabled to serve the purpose of the organization. The NMM offers a set of process related questions that deal with these issues, so that by answering these, the leaders can establish good processes for their organizations (Figure 4.1).

Nonprofit organizations have to routinely work with multiple constituents. Nonprofits' financial resources, in many cases, depend on their ability to raise funds from donors. In addition to serving their constituents, to thrive they have to keep the trust of their donors, win the commitment of their employees, and often even collaborate with all other organizations that serve the same constituency. In this chapter, we elaborate four common processes found in nonprofits: decision-making power; leadership authority; listening skills to engage and gain support; and fund-raising.

Case Study: Advocacy Nation I

Advocacy Nation was a nonprofit organization dedicated to political advocacy for a particular group of people who were discriminated against and needed better legal and social representation in the mainstream of the nation. After the founding leader of the organization left, the board discovered that she had managed to alienate a key group of donors, which led to financial constraints that threatened its operations. Monica was the board member who volunteered to lead the search for a new leader, with the hope of remedying the financial situation. Monica's full-time paid work was in the Consumer Research of a well-know international corporate entity. In her description, she explained that the hiring process for the new leader for Advocacy Nation surprised her. It was in sharp contrast to her experience in the corporate sector. The search process led to hundreds of hours of gathering input from a diverse group of stakeholders, in order to establish the key criteria to be used in the search for the next Executive Director. The board met with employees, key donors, the prominent members of the group they advocated for, and other stakeholders in the community. Monica worked with the board to create a 50-person Community Panel to define a job description and an appropriate recruitment process. Each step had to be reviewed by the panel for approval. Although there were no staff members on the search panel initially, when Advocacy

Nation had narrowed it to two final candidates the staff interviewed them as well. The staff felt it was important to have a voice in the final hiring decision. These extensive discussions and forums were conducted over a period of nine months during which time the organization remained without an active leader. It was through these discussions and meetings that the problems with the previous leader's approach to a subgroup of important donors were uncovered. It was through this consultative process that it became clear how important the personal skills of the individual in the leadership role were for the future success of the organization. In the various criteria for selecting the new candidate for the job, one important agreement was that it would have to be a candidate who had the qualities needed to woo back the alienated group of donors, on whom the organization counted for a reasonable part of its budget.

This led to another important question for Advocacy Nation: How will you raise funds to support your purpose? Monica described how the importance of a single person, and the search for the right person for the role, was important enough to have involved hundreds of people-hours of discussion and deliberation over an elapsed time of three-quarters of a year. She opined that a similar leadership role in a business organization would not lie vacant for more than nine days, in sharp contrast to the nine months it took for Advocacy Nation. For Advocacy Nation, as with other similar nonprofits, the decision-making process had to include input from external stakeholders, donors as well as beneficiaries, and the employees who felt they had to have a voice in what qualities would make a successful leader for the organization they affiliated with. The pace of decision-making was dictated by the recognition of the importance of the individual. A process had to be designed that took into account input from all the stakeholders, including staff, since people matter in a nonprofit context in more ways than in a for-profit organization.

Decision-making

In a *Stanford Social Innovation Review* article, "What Business Execs Don't Know—but Should—About Nonprofits,"[1] Harold Williams, who worked as a CEO for for-profits and nonprofits, advised nonprofit leaders, "You will have little opportunity to lead by making decisions.

You'll have the power of the budget to some extent, but if you have a vision or you want to make changes, you're going to do it by leadership and by inspiration and not by direction. You've got to be the Pied Piper." The case of Advocacy Nation illustrates the importance of process. The organization only had a permanent staff of a little over a dozen people. Yet the political advocacy responsibility it carried made it one of the most powerful advocacy organizations in the state. The nine-month-long consultative approach to hiring an executive director for this organization is not unusual in the world of nonprofits. A business manager may dismiss this as simply inefficient operations, but a deeper understanding of the operations of such an organization shows why a faster business-like hiring decision-making process is not relevant or appropriate for such a position.

Legislative Versus Executive Power

Jim Collins, the author of the monograph called *Good to Great and the Social Sectors*, a companion to the best-selling book *Good to Great: Why Some Companies Make the Leap ... and Others Don't*, recognized the need for a different approach in the social sectors. In the monograph he articulates that the sources of a leader's power in for-profit and not-for-profit organizations are fundamentally different. He offers a distinction between executive and legislative powers, proposing that for-profit leaders have executive powers while nonprofit leaders have legislative powers. The executive power is the ability to reward and punish based on being higher up in the hierarchical structure of a business organization. The legislative power does not rely on material rewards or positional ability to impose punitive measures. Nonprofit leaders may not have a hierarchical organization—as a number of them tend to have a flat, networked structure, where legislative power is more useful instead.

In the same monograph, Frances Hesselbein, the CEO of the Girl Scouts of the USA, describes her position as being "in the center of an organization, as opposed to being at the top" as she accomplishes her goals using influence rather than direct power.[2] Nonprofit leaders do not have access to the same executive or reward power as that available to leaders in the corporate world. They must rely on processes where they can get the same effective collective action as any other organization, without the power to punish or reward. One skill they use effectively is to listen. The leaders

Figure 4.2. Executive For-profit versus Legislative Nonprofit power.[3]

we studied were all describing activities that were routine for them, which involved listening to all different stakeholders.

Listening Skills

Kenneth Branagh, actor/director from Northern Ireland, when asked by a radio interviewer, "what has being an actor/director taught you about leadership?", responded: "I think that it is continuing to teach me and it is an evolving process that I find is mostly to do in my case with listening more, listening more and more and more. 'Give all men thine ear but few thy voice,' as Shakespeare says."

> I don't do it for them [the actors]. I don't need to bring the things they bring. I can't. I can't do their job. I need not to do their job. It's not my job to do their job. My job is to create conditions in which they can do their job as well as possible and I think to give back maximum value as enjoyably as possible. It will always be dramatic. There will always be passion. There will always be ups and downs. But if you can, as it were, direct the context in which that work happens. That involves a great deal of listening. Then I think strides can be made.[4]
>
> Kenneth Branagh speaking on KQED Radio's *Forum*, April 27, 2012

The primary focus of leadership training in textbooks is on the role of the leader as the one to create a vision, communicate it, and inspire the

Table 4.1. Leadership Behaviors

Leadership Behaviors
Establish goals and timelines
Establish methods of evaluation: Establish high standard of excellence
Problem solving
Strong role model
Define roles: Clarify what is to be done, how it is to be done, who is responsible to do it. Giving directions.
Motivate subordinates: Challenge subordinates to perform at highest level possible. Demonstrate confidence in their capabilities. Consult with subordinates to obtain their ideas and opinions.

followers, sometimes with charisma, to achieve collective action for meeting some goals. Table 4.1 provides a list of common leadership behaviors, pared down to major categories, complied from several academic articles on leadership. Listening is an important leadership activity and yet the theories never mention it. The quote by Kenneth Branagh makes it clear that, in practice, it is recognized that listening is an essential leadership tool.

Through our research interviews with several leaders of nonprofit organizations we identified that listening was an important activity. We asked the leaders for detailed and specific examples of their work focusing them on their current projects, initiatives, or day-to-day activities that were taking up their time. We categorized these activities around the concepts derived from leadership theory, as listed in Table 4.1. These analytic efforts made us aware that many of the leaders were describing activities that involved listening. However, this key tool for leaders was not a part of the leadership traits that we had identified from the leadership literature.

Our data showed that leaders spend a lot of their time in various situations that require them to be actively listening. So much so that it was evident that this is an important leadership activity that deserved to be listed explicitly alongside the others in Table 4.1. The last activity listed in Table 4.1, "Consult with subordinates," implied a listening role for the leader, but more often communication is focused on the leader trying to sell his ideas to the followers.

In describing their day-to-day activities, the leaders we interviewed revealed how a lot of what they did was essentially "to listen." They needed to find out what their employees, donors, collaborators, customers, policy makers, boards, and various other stakeholders needed or wanted. This focus on listening was so pervasive in their descriptions that we are surprised that the academic research on leadership does not list listening as an essential, or at the very least one of, the traits or skills for leaders.

Theories of leadership indirectly imply listening as being important, as several leadership activities like communication, consulting, and gathering input, require listening. However, there is no explicit focus on listening. Even the communication models offered to leaders do not mention listening. The communication models focus on coding the message and selecting the appropriate channel for communicating the message. The underlying assumption in these is that the leader is primarily in a broadcast mode, rather than in a role to listen or enter into a dialogue. These leadership theories seem to be completely divorced from the experiential descriptions of what leaders say they are really doing. All the nonprofit leaders described spending a lot of their time gathering input and simply listening to people within and outside their organizations.

We propose that listening is an essential skill for a leader. After all, the leader articulates the aspirations of a collective of followers, much greater in strength of sheer numbers, and to be able to do that with any authenticity the leader needs to be a good listener and an empathetic one, too. Our data shows that listening really well is what allows a leader to capture the zeitgeist and the collective aspirations of the followers. The leaders do not have any special skills like mindreading or clairvoyance or wizardry of any kind, yet are able to capture the imagination of their followers and articulate their collective aspirations because they have the ability to listen and pay attention to the content and emotion of what they hear.

Case Study: Partners Developing Communities from the Inside

One example of the importance of the leader's listening skills was from a community development organization. Lakeesha, the leader, was the director of a community development organization called Partners Developing Communities (PDC). Lakeesha travelled overseas from the United States to countries in Africa in order to understand how development work was undertaken in other parts of the world. The biggest lesson she came back with was that the very concept of "development" was questionable. She noticed that the communities that thrived in Africa, despite being poverty stricken, were not dependent on help from outside for their "development." The community members took responsibility for their own development. They recognized and accepted that no one from the outside was going to save them and that they had to help themselves with whatever resources they already had.

On her return, she radically shifted and refocused PDC. The emphasis was now placed on community engagement instead of just development. Community engagement was center stage because it was seen as the way to produce development that was enduring. Before her trip, PDC was focused on bringing services and resources into low-income community. After the trip, she asked herself the important question: How can I leverage my organization's success to improve our ability to make a difference? She reorganized the focus and processes of PDC to listen to the community members, to understand their strengths and contributions, and to support them individually. Building an interconnected community to help each other with mutual support was a pathway for the group to thrive.

Case Study: Listening to an Organization

Martina was the leader of a large civic department that had a long history of being very hierarchical. Martina enjoyed extensive executive powers and could command loyalty and obedience from those who reported to her based purely on the traditional training and socialization into their roles from historical precedent. The stereotypical image of the organization was one of a strict hierarchy where the chain of command was maintained with deference. A typical leader in such an organization may be expected to sit behind a desk and draft Policies and Procedures. Martina chose to spent about 10% of her work time in situations where she was interacting with her constituents and the population her organization served. She had asked herself: How can I communicate with stakeholders? She listened to them and learned that her organization was perceived as a bureaucracy and her employees that dealt with the constituents were not well liked, despite being in a role that was supposed to be a helpful one. She wanted to change that.

Martina aspired for her organization to be seen and admired by the community for its helpful role. As part of learning more about her organization, beyond the formal reports and meetings, she set up a monthly open forum where anyone from the 90 employees and the 65 volunteers could come. Regardless of their position in the organizational hierarchy, anyone could come to these monthly forums and raise any issues they wanted to bring to her attention. The forums were a way for her to listen to her employees and provide them with direct access to the leader, bypassing the more traditional channels of the bureaucratic organization. These forums became a way for many suggestions and ideas to gradually grow into processes that put the organization on the path to serving the community better, and being admired for it.

Using Values to Engage

Listening is a prerequisite to building engagement. The values and mission of an organization can only be realized with engaged stakeholders. We want to point out that the leaders were not just listening to provide only what the various stakeholders were asking for, or even to build consensus. They were listening to pay attention, to really understand empathetically what the real concern was, and to find a way to address that concern without compromising on the main goal, vision, and values that were critical to bringing these different stakeholders into the conversation. Leaders listened and used their own values or their organizations' missions to construct dialogue and shared understanding that allowed them to be effective leaders. From Patrick's example in Chapter 1, he used his clarity of the purpose to redirect the board and staff when one staff member asked for each program to have a surplus, instead of examining its purpose within the greater organization.

Fund-raising

The manner in which nonprofit organizations fund their services is radically different from the way a typical business funds its operations, and this is an area where there is a lot of room for mistaken assumptions on all sides. Some people are just surprised to know that even nonprofits need to generate money, simply to support the program and administrative costs (including personnel, services, and materials) they provide. They just have not thought about the monetary aspects, or assume that the resources are volunteered. Several nonprofits even generate earned income, which is permissible by regulations, as long as the profits are used only to support the primary purpose and related programs of the organization. Nonprofits potentially could have excess cash. The US government regulations allow the earning of income and holding excess cash; however, the regulations prevent a nonprofit organization from issuing stock. Thus, nonprofit organizations do not have access to capital from equity markets for long-term investments.

The main sources of capital funding available to any nonprofit fall into one of the following four funding categories:

1. Grant Seeker Model—where the majority of income is received by requesting significant charitable donations from private institutional funders, corporate foundations, and individual donors
2. Local and/or foreign government support
3. Self-sustaining through revenue generation
4. Grants from global human services programs

These are representative, not comprehensive, ways of financing nonprofit organizations and many organizations use some combination of these funding sources. In fact, many organizations find a diversification of sources can provide their organization stability during challenging economic times. Often, grant-giving foundations will have clauses for the grantee nonprofits to generate a portion of their funding needs by independent fundraising efforts, membership collections, or even revenue from charging nominal fees for their services or other aspects of their operations. Several nonprofits rely on revenue from their products and services for their operating expenses. According to the National Nonprofit Research Database, in 2004 charities received their income from the following sources: Fees for Service, 70.9%; Private Contributions, 12.5%; Government Grants, 9%; Investment Income, 3.9%; and Other Income, 3.7%.

Monica, the board member from Advocacy Nation, who also had a full time corporate job, described the relentless pursuit of funding for the nonprofit to be a real contrast between her two worlds. She said that when people work for a company they tend to follow the vision set out by the CEO and the top management, and the funding is arranged by the top management—typically by the people in-charge of the finance or treasury function. In Advocacy Nation, she found that this fund-raising role fell on the executive director. The leader, in the nonprofit context, had to be a program manager. They typically had to budget and spend almost half their time "chasing dollars" and accounting for it to the donors. Leaders also had to continuously find donors who supported their cause. One leader estimated that this could take 50% of his work time.

One nonprofit leader described the delicate balance of satisfying the goals of funders while maintaining the values and goals of the organization: "You have to pay attention to what they give money to and what they want you to do. The art of fund-raising is to interpret what you do within the confines of what funders want you to do. Funders control the game. This is the program we do and it accomplishes your mission by … and then they'll give you money. This is not a negative—just the way of the world, they control the purse strings."

Case Study: Paying for Hospice Care in India*

India's population of over one billion had a large percentage of citizens who lacked access to healthcare. Of the one million new cancer cases that were diagnosed each year, 80% were in an incurable stage. Due to the changes brought about by breakneck economic development, the traditional Indian extended family fragmented into nuclear families, leaving many old people, who would have previously been cared for by their children, being left to die alone and without any system to care for them. There was an unmet need for hospice care to serve the hundreds of thousands of people suffering from chronic and terminal illness. Hospice and palliative care could help them to die with dignity and free of pain. Brthya was a charitable organization that provided hospice care in Chennai, India. It was looking for ways to expand its operations to other parts of the country, and perhaps other developing countries around the

* Case study based on research with Dr. Shyam Kamath.

world, in a manner that could be sustained. It had a partner nonprofit in the US, Add Value to Life (AVTL), which helped raise funds for their efforts. The AVTL-Brthya organization wanted to find ways to expand its operations viably.

Hospice care focused on the full spiritual, cultural, psychological, emotional, and social needs of the patient, family, and community, since those involved defined and drove the care they considered to be appropriate. Given the understanding that the patient's condition was not expected to improve, care was focused on compassionate management of the condition, with the goal to maximize the quality of life. It involved monitoring treatment, therapy and medications to reduce pain or address other items that could be treated, attending to the patients' comfort including activities to prevent or reduce bedsores, etc. Another component of hospice care was to educate, consult, and provide facilities, financing, and grief assistance, right down to funeral planning and bereavement assistance to the family and community after the death of the patient.

Hospice care providers were organized in four different ways, based on how they provide care and manage their operations. These were (a) home hospice care, (b) facility hospice care, (c) combined hospice care, and (d) network hospice care.

Hospices could be funded many different ways, some of which were: patients and their family pay for service; insurance; government grants supporting hospice care facilities as nonprofit social services; nongovernment organization (NGO) grants; charity; endowment funds; corporate partnerships; or hospital cost shifting. The most common sources of funding for independent hospice operations—whether they were home hospice, facility hospice, or both—were charities, NGO grants, and corporate sponsorships. AVTL-Brthya wasn't certain how to maintain ongoing sources of funding the hospice care needed, especially for the vast number of those who could not afford to pay for it.

Nonprofits are continually challenged to create a variety of income streams to support programming that cannot generate enough earned revenue from the underprivileged, under-resourced clients they served. As they face the revenue challenges described in Chapter 2, they must regularly ask themselves: How can we raise funds to support our purpose?

They must be prepared to try different revenue-generating processes to balance shrinking endowments, decreased government funding, or increased client needs. In another case, of Workforce Development, described below, it became clear that a sound revenue-generating strategy wasn't enough to deal with a sudden economic downturn.

Case Study: Improving the Bottom Line at Workforce Development USA

Workforce Development USA had a network of over 150 community-based chapters throughout North America that offered training and development for job placement, while operating retail stores for donated goods. One regional West Coast chapter alone had over 500 employees, and operated more than a dozen retail stores in several counties. In 2009, this multicounty chapter generated 69% of the revenue needed to support its programs in education, training and employment. This nonprofit organization, with a budget of over $32 million, was deeply affected by the national economic downturn. The first major blow to the organization's cash flow was caused by the failed sale of its headquarters in July 2008, which was in final contract status when the buyer defaulted due to the unfolding credit crisis. This resulted in a loss of $6 million in investment capital and nearly $1 million in operating capital. Since then, the revenues it counted on from the sale of salvage materials, such as metal and wood, plummeted with the drop in world commodity prices. And, like many nonprofits across the country, the organization's grant income was threatened by the significant drop in foundation portfolio values. The leadership team was facing a projected deficit of $3 million.

At the same time, demand for Workforce Development USA's free job-training and placement services skyrocketed—with monthly attendance at five times the projections. Although Workforce Development USA's revenue could cover its operations, even in good economic times it did not provide enough income to fulfill its mission: to encourage economic self-sufficiency by providing job training and counseling to overcome barriers to employment. Like all nonprofits, it was the mission that was the focus of its financial planning, not the profit bottom line. The management team knew that they needed to bring in more revenue to meet the urgent need.

Between October 2008 and January 2009, the leadership team tapped their combined creativity and passion for Workforce Development USA's mission to reduce the $3 million deficit to $1 million, without impacting services. However, to maintain Workforce Development USA's high standards for quality service and meet the demand created by the nation's highest monthly unemployment growth rate in 60 years, Workforce Development USA launched the first ever fund-raising campaign in its nearly 100-year history. They knew that an individual donor campaign is an ambitious project in a recessionary economy. However, during these trying economic times, the leadership team had two options: raise an additional $1 million from individual donors to fill the budget gap; or reduce the critical services that the organization provided. The organization had to bolster the financial resources—to achieve the organization's mission, which was needed more than ever in the wake of the economic downturn.

In order to improve a nonprofit organization's delivery of its purpose, we recommend focusing on processes. As can be seen in the case studies described in this chapter, helpful processes can focus on decision-making power; leadership authority; listening skills to engage and gain support; and diversified and flexible fund-raising. Business organizations tend to have hierarchical reporting structures with executive powers to reward or punish those lower down the hierarchy. Nonprofits are more likely to have flatter networked forms with legislative powers where people need to be persuaded with influence toward consensus-based decisions. Nonprofit leaders thus need to have many ways to listen to and engage their various stakeholders. Successful nonprofits design processes that include their diverse stakeholders: employees, donors, clients, and other stakeholders. The processes support the purpose of the organization and enable cooperation amongst the people who have come together to make it successful. Chapter 5 explains the ways in which people are key to an organization's success.

CHAPTER 5

People Before Systems

People make organizations. As employees, suppliers, customers, regulators, and founders, among many other roles, they make up the ecosystem in which the organization is enacted. In proposing the PPP model, what do we mean when we recommend using a people-focused approach to managing a nonprofit? How, if at all, is it different from the way people are managed in a business organization? This chapter has the answers and examples for why nonprofit organizations need to do some things differently than businesses when it comes to managing people. The model in Figure 5.1 illustrates the key guiding questions that will be helpful to nonprofits as they focus on the people in the organization, and their collective ability to support the basic purpose of the organization.

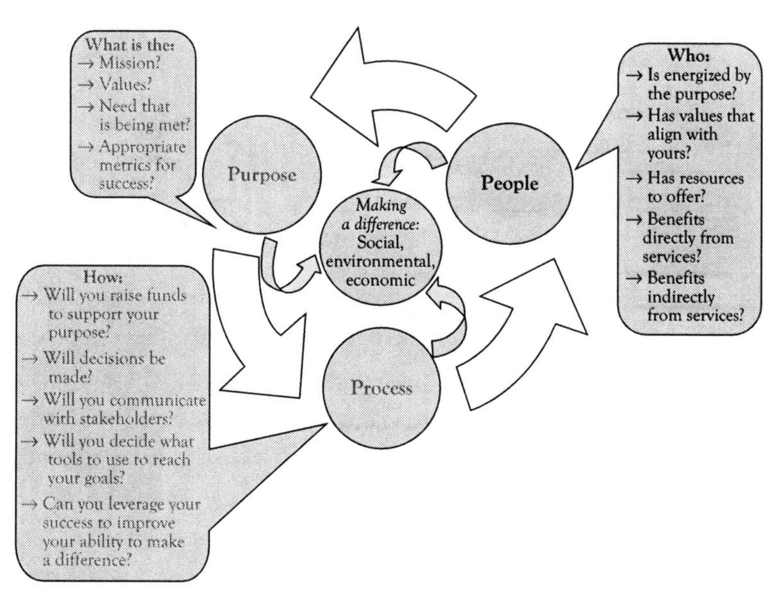

Figure 5.1. Nonprofit management model: People.

In business organizations, management systems are used to channel the collective action of people. There are contracts for all types of transactions and for guiding mutual expectations. There are controls in place to ensure behavior and process complaints. These ensure that no single individual has an unduly large influence in the organization and there are penalty clauses in contracts in case of nondelivery or noncompliance. These same management practices are also useful for managing nonprofits, and are indeed commonly used. However, with better appreciation of the differences that separate nonprofit organizations from business enterprises, these systems and practices can be made more applicable with some modifications better fit nonprofits.

The NMM prescribes that a people-focused approach is more effective in nonprofit organizations. We will illustrate what this means and how it plays out with some examples. In Chapter 3, we described how business and nonprofit organizations are similar in some respects and different in others. Since these underlying differences are the reason that nonprofits need a modified set of systems and practices, let us look at some of these differences and their implications for managing organizations effectively.

In a business organization, the leader typically is at the top of a hierarchical organization whereas in a nonprofit, the leader is at the center of an organizational network. This also translates into the business leader having executive power whereas the nonprofit leaders have legislative power through the influence they may be able to have over the network. This is illustrated with the case study about Advocacy Nation.

Case Study: Advocacy Nation II

The Advocacy Nation organization was introduced earlier as the nonprofit organization dedicated to political advocacy for a particular group of people who were discriminated against and needed better legal and social representation in the mainstream life of the nation. A former executive director had managed to alienate a key group of donors, leading to significantly lower donations. The organization was without a leader and the board had agreed that a new leader would need to be hired. After extensive discussions and forums lasting several months, a new executive director was hired.

The importance of the particular individual in the executive director role became clearer as only the right candidate would be able to woo back the alienated group of donors, who contributed a substantial part of its budget. The importance of a single person, and the search for the right person for the role, was important enough to devote nine months to deliberation before hiring. A similar leadership role in a business organization would not lie vacant for more than nine days. The pace of decision-making was set by this important consideration, which is seldom seen in a typical business hiring situation.

Advocacy Nation only had a permanent staff of a little over a dozen full-time people. Yet the political advocacy responsibility it carried made it one of the most powerful advocacy organizations in the state. The nine-month-long consultative approach to hiring an executive director for this organization is not extraordinary in the world of nonprofits, although in a business organization this would be considered inordinately slow. In a business organization of similar size, the process would be a lot simpler and the decision-maker would move right along to replace the position within days, rather than months. There would be no need for any consultations with stakeholders outside the firm as their approval of the executive director would not be needed at all.

A chief executive officer of a medium-sized business, who heard about this situation at Advocacy Nation, was shocked initially. After he was told about the way Advocacy Nation was different from a similar-sized business organization, he found it particularly useful in making him appreciate the difference between his business world and his role on the nonprofit board he served on. He declared that learning about these differences made the long consultative hiring process seem more reasonable given the context although it would still be outrageous in the business world that he operated in. In his capacity as the chief executive officer of a mid-sized business, this consultative approach would be quite out of the question. It would be the equivalent of him going to his bankers to ask whether a particular chief financial officer would be acceptable to the bankers who loaned to the business. He did not see any business ever having to do that.

Another difference between nonprofits and businesses is how leaders in the former rely on exerting influence while in the latter power may be used more readily than influence. This difference, too, plays out in how nonprofits thrive better with a people-centric approach. Let us show this through a case study.

Case Study: Vision 2020

The founder of a youth development organization, Hopeful Frontiers, hired a chief operating officer (COO) for his medium-sized nonprofit organization. The COO, Jeff, was hired because of his successful career in a well-known global business organization. For Jeff, this was part of his mid-career transition. He was drawn by the chance to work with the well-respected founder and by the mission of Hopeful Frontiers that served youth throughout a large region. The organization had a staff of 15 people who served 80,000 students annually. Jeff was excited to join because the organization was poised for growth.

Jeff brought a wealth of experience in making good judgment calls in the face of many managerial dilemmas that are common in organizational environments. He knew how to define and articulate managerial problems and was effective at communicating them to get others involved in solving them. While still new in his role, he created a growth strategy to spread the program to other communities. He assumed that everyone agreed that growth was good and that such a plan would inspire and energize the employees. From his previous business experience, a specific target-oriented growth strategy motivated employees and aligned their actions to help achieve the corporate objectives. With the Hopeful Frontiers management team, they created an expansion structure designed to serve one million school students in 20 cities by 2020. He expected his staff to embrace this plan with the same enthusiasm that his plans had met with in his business roles earlier. To his surprise, the staff members hated it.

When he presented his vision of growth for Hopeful Frontiers, he was shocked to discover that the employees were opposed to it. He had anticipated some resistance to change, but there was a coup. There was no one who showed any excitement about his vision, and there were many who were openly critical of this plan. They called it, "growth for growth's sake." They spoke up in the meeting, declaring their concerns about how this growth would negatively impact the quality of the programs. They were also concerned that many of the employees, who actually delivered the programs in the schools, would have to travel to schools far away from their home districts. This growth also raised the possibility that some of them might be transferred to new locations, where they were not interested in going.

Jeff listened intently to their concerns and agreed to reconsider the strategy. He knew it had to be withdrawn as presented. As he talked more with them, he learned how many of the employees who worked for the nonprofit were doing so at the cost of what many would consider a personal sacrifice in monetary compensation. Many of the employees did this because they believed that the mission of the organization gave them a chance to bring and express their values through their work. Some of them settled for the lower salary in the nonprofit because they felt that by forgoing the higher salary at a corporation they were also forgoing the pressures that came with it, be that to commute long distances, work long hours, or be required to grow at a certain pace.

When confronted with employee dissatisfaction towards the strategy he proposed, Jeff stepped back to ask himself: How is the staff energized by the purpose? In his words, "We forgot that the staff was there for the mission." In order to motivate and engage the employees and volunteers, he had to find a way to align the organizational goals with the personal motivations of the people who worked for the organization. Taking the employees' concerns into consideration, he revised his strategy. He and the management team created new processes to regularly listen to his staff. Then they reformulated the growth vision to be more consistent with the organization's key resource, its people. The revised strategy focused less on target numbers and more on the societal impact they would be making. He kept the goal of bringing this great program to more students, and created a two-year pilot process (expanding only to three cities initially): 20,000 more students in two years. This gave him time to build trust and buy-in with the staff and communities, and to focus his message on the mission and metrics that motivated people.

In our conversation with Jeff, he also described how he had to reflect on his personal value of "growth," and how it related to and impacted the collective values of the organization. The personal values of the leader and how he shapes the organizational values is a critical aspect of nonprofit organizations. In nonprofit organizations the followership matters just as much as the leadership. The leader's challenge is to engage the followers.

One way to do this is to be transparent as a leader in setting clear direction and ethical policies that are implemented in an exemplary manner, in order to earn the respect and loyalty of the followers. Let us look at this through another case study.

Case Study: Walking the Talk

We told you the story of Martina, the leader of a hierarchical government department in chapter 4, in the case study titled Listening to an Organization. Her department had a budget of $10 million a year, with 100 employees and 65 volunteers. As part of a leadership development retreat, she spent a great deal of time reflecting on her personal values and how, if at all, she expressed them in her life. Her three most important personal values were:

1. Fitness—physical, spiritual, mental
2. Authentic leadership—boundaries, honesty with others and self
3. Contentment—balance, action/words, enjoyment

She wanted her values to be expressed through her work. As a daily reminder and to let people know what she stood for, she put a framed copy of these values in a visible location in her office. She let it be known that she intended to act in accordance with these values. She used the people-focused questions from the NMM about values, and used alignment with values as a guiding management principle. She steered the management team of her department in creating explicit values for the organization. These organizational values were posted near the elevator and other parts of the office premises where everyone could see them easily. She actively practiced living by these values by making clear and consistent decisions that would allow everyone to see that she was walking the talk.

The real test came when a very competent and trusted officer of her department made a mistake. He could have been forgiven or treated as everyone else in the department and reprimanded for the mistake. Ordinarily, in the absence of written values, he would likely have been forgiven based on his stellar reputation. However, with the displayed values and the public commitment to enact these consistently, this officer was reprimanded exactly the same as anyone else in his shoes would have. Some may consider this approach to be unduly harsh and strict. However, for the organization as whole, this uniformity helped send a powerful message that values were important, and would be applied impartially for all. For Martina, the written values helped resolve the dilemma. Her goal was to ensure that the organization as a whole delivered fairness and justice for everyone equally. Such a value-centric approach is important for all organizations, and it is critical for the people-centric nonprofit organizations.

In making every decision align with her values, Martina was able to "live her values" through her day-to-day actions. It became clear that these actions were critical to her ability to lead effectively. She said that if she was to move decision-making down through the traditionally hierarchical organization, she had to allow people to see that she meant it. In pushing decision-making down the organization, Martina told her employees that if what they were doing was not illegal, unethical, or against policy and was consistent with the organization's mission, they did not need to wait to get permission to do it. This gave individuals responsibility for their actions and increased the response time to make the organization less bureaucratic for their customers. Martina's objective was to be as transparent in her own decision-making as possible, so her stated values, as posted in her office, were seen in her actions by her employees. This allowed her to model the behavior she expected from the employees.

Assuming organizations to be social entities with many other goals, rather than just the economic goal of maximizing profit, helps managers make more effective decisions. Organizations are social entities, too; they cultivate reputations for being a good place to work, or responsible community actors who participate as good citizens. People tend to find jobs with organizations that are in fields related to their interests and passions. They express themselves through their work. There are social interactions in organizations with bonds of friendship, enmity, and all manner of relationship. The employees care about the organizations in which they spend large parts of their waking lives. People are not perfectly rational replaceable parts that make up an organization.

We participate in organizational life, bringing all the complexities of humanness into the situation. People work for many different reasons in addition to the need to make money and take pride in making a difference through their professional achievements (Figure 5.2).

Figure 5.2. Employee motivation.[1]

Consider this example: one of the people we interviewed left a university department to work for a business company that sold software to universities. While she respected the owner's business acumen, she found that he was challenged to understand what would make a university employee choose his software. Unlike for-profit staff, nonprofit employees did not have the same incentives. The salesman had to understand the intangibles that made the jobs special for the people who worked in a nonprofit. They wanted to contribute to something meaningful. They wanted to go home and feel good about what they did. The informality and camaraderie in a department were very important—as was the support of worklife balance. It was not just about making the numbers, but helping people understand how they contributed to society. A university employee is less likely to choose a piece of software on the basis of cost and efficiency and more likely to do so on the basis of reputation and effectiveness.

CHAPTER 6
The Key Lessons

The goal of strategy in nonprofit organizations is to effectively deliver the cause for which the nonprofit exists. For a business, strategy is about gaining competitive advantage. For nonprofits, the competition is not about their cause because if another nonprofit is serving the same social need, then they may even collaborate or support each other, rather than compete. A number of social causes served by nonprofits are such that the demand for services far exceeds their supply. Nonprofit organizations need ways to deliver their goods and services more effectively. Our motivation in writing this book was to provide leaders of nonprofit organizations a set of business-derived tools that will help them make and implement better strategy for their organizations. This chapter is a summary of the key lessons from the book.

There is a tacit assumption made by many business leaders that the same management principles that have made them successful in business can be effectively used to manage nonprofit organizations as well. When these managers serve on boards or in advisory roles for nonprofit organizations, they offer advice and direction that is based on their business expertise. Often they are major donors to these organizations, too. Their advice is taken rather seriously, out of deference for their role as board members in the organizational hierarchy and also because the nonprofit organization depends on their generosity for funding.

The executive directors of nonprofit organizations feel a fiduciary responsibility toward their donors and listen intently for direction from the business leaders working with them. The experienced executive directors sometimes report feeling that their business partners do not really understand the nonprofit world. Some even feel angry that they are treated as if they don't know the right things to do, while the advisors have all the answers. The less-experienced executive directors take the advice and implement it, often to discover that it is not always sound or reliable and, mostly, it does not address the issues they face. Some executive directors report being so disillusioned that they only follow these board recommendations as a way to appease the board members; for example, sitting through management training that they privately consider a total waste of time.

Our research challenges the tacit assumption that business principles apply to nonprofits. We offer the board members from a business background and the executive directors of nonprofit organizations a set of tools for managing nonprofit organizations. The NMM is derived from the business strategy tool kit. It modifies business practices to better suit the nonprofit context. It will help executive directors to explain their organizations and strategies to their stakeholders in language that is business friendly.

If you are leading a nonprofit organization and work with donors or board members who ask you to adopt some business practice or other, you can assess whether that is appropriate to do or not. In order to do that, you can use the list of differences between business and nonprofits that is presented in Chapter 2 and assess if these differences will matter for adopting that particular practice. If it seems that they won't, then adopt the business practice. If it seems that there are good reasons why the practice should not be adopted, then use the list of differences as a way to educate your collaborators from the business world. Often they have no idea why it does not make sense for your organization to adopt that practice. They may never have considered how nonprofits are different, and it is left to the nonprofit leaders to articulate these differences. Executive directors of nonprofit organizations have the responsibility to communicate the importance of these differences for the purpose of managing these organizations.

In summary, the key differences between nonprofit and business enterprises are that: (1) Nonprofits service a cause at a cost, while businesses serve products or services to be profitable. (2) Nonprofits are successful if they achieve their purpose which should be measured by metrics that can get to assessments of social change at cost-effective levels, while businesses are successful if they achieve growth and profitability, typically measured with financial metrics. (3) Nonprofits tend to attract employees who care about the cause or work environment or lifestyle choices, while businesses may attract employees who are more focused on personal and professional achievements measured by financial and career growth. (4) Nonprofits have leaders who are at the center of a network, with legislative-style influence over the enterprise while business leaders are more often at the top of a hierarchy with executive powers to reward and punish others within the enterprise. (5) Nonprofits have to constantly raise funds to provide their services while a business can become self-sustaining after its products and services are generating profits or its market capitalization is funding its growth. (6) Nonprofits tend to become embedded in the communities that they operate in and do not have the same freedom to relocate or close operations as a business in the same context has, since local stakeholders are more important for nonprofits. (7) Nonprofits usually operate in an environment of scarcity and operate with a sense of fiduciary responsibility toward their funders and donors, while businesses are comparatively more resource rich and have the goal to enrich their shareholders, who are considered willing partners in the risk-taking ventures of the enterprise. (8) Nonprofit enterprises serve unmet societal needs for which the demand frequently outstrips scarce supply, and they have to turn away the needy who come to seek their help. There is no need to create demand by advertising or marketing the social services in the manner that businesses have to generate demand for their products and services. (9) Nonprofits face competition in the fund-raising arena where they chase the same donors and foundations for a share of their charity dollars. If there are other nonprofits serving the same social need, they seldom compete, and more often cooperate towards attaining the shared social changes.

Given these differences, the strategic management frameworks developed for businesses are neither appropriate nor particularly useful for managing nonprofit organizations. The business-style operation through strategy-structure-systems approach is not as effective as a social approach focused on purpose-process-people. The basic assumption behind the SSS framework is that organizations are profit-maximizing economic entities, which applies to businesses but is irrelevant for nonprofit organizations. Nonprofit organizations are mission and values driven, hence the PPP approach is more appropriate for them.

The nonprofit sector is an important and growing contributor to the US economy. It supplies an increasing proportion of employment and essential services. Business and nonprofit organizations are alike in some ways since they are organized ways for people to work together and accomplish as a group what they would not be able to achieve as individuals. There is need for some coordinating mechanisms to achieve collective actions toward shared objectives. For nonprofits, this is better achieved with a purpose-process-people focus where a business may rely on strategy-structure-systems.

There are many different ways to describe the purpose of an enterprise, such as the cause, values, mission, or the social need that it fulfills. It is hard to quantify the purpose for measuring it as an output. Yet a clearly articulated purpose guides everyone within and outside the organization on a day-to-day basis as they make their operational decisions. One way to check if an organization has a well-defined purpose is to ask if it is articulated in a manner that allows people within and outside to know what the enterprise does. Another way to check if the purpose is articulated properly is to check if it applies to other organizations or not. If a statement of purpose can be transferred to another organization and it still seems applicable, then it is not adequately specified and needs more refinement. For example, is a mission statement that says "provide excellent service at a reasonable cost" a good mission statement? It is an excellent goal but it is not a good enough statement of purpose—because it applies equally well to most organizations and does not distinguish the mission of your organization from that of others. It needs to be more specific and unique, so that employees, donors, clients and others can all read it and know what your organization stands for, and what to expect.

It is also useful to develop measures to quantify and track the goals spelled out in the statement of purpose It is better to have some measures, even if approximate or subjective, than to have none, as the simple act of keeping track can improve performance. The answers to the questions proposed in the NMM—what is the mission, what are the values of the organization, what needs does it serve, and how would the success be measured—are a good starting point to establish a dialogue about the purpose of the organization and to develop metrics to track the purpose. While articulating the mission statement is a onetime event, it takes several coordinated decisions and actions over time to translate that mission into the realized purpose. These enactments of mission can be guided to stay on track by asking the questions in the model at each major decision point.

Business organizations have a capital structure (equity, debt, loans, etc) while nonprofits have a fund-raising process. Nonprofit funding can come from grants, foundations, donations, etc. Business organizations tend to have hierarchical reporting structures with executive powers to reward or punish those lower down the hierarchy. In contrast, nonprofits need communication processes that work across flatter networked organizational forms. The processes are also important to exert legislative powers, where people need to be persuaded with influence toward consensus-based decisions.

Processes are the preferred way to manage nonprofits. Structures can be rigid and expensive since they may require investments in staff, training, systems, and maintaining these. Nonprofits tend to rely on a more flexible approach with volunteer and part-time staff, who are better engaged with processes that can be modified without costly retraining. The questions in the NMM model—such as how will the participants communicate and how will the organization raise funds—are a good way to develop and establish some processes.

Nonprofits have to rely more on people-centered approaches as people matter a lot more in this context. In business organizations, people are often treated as being dispensable more readily as their skills are more transferable. In nonprofits, people bring their passion for the cause and are thus not as replaceable. There is a self-selection process at work as people with certain values tend to select organizations with consistent missions (goals and values) where they can express these values in realizing the shared goals. Questions in the NMM model are one possible way to identify the right people and deploy them for the correct purpose. Such consistency in personal and organizational values tends to create enterprises with a greater level of engagement than a typical business organization.

In using management practices that are in consonance with their cultural context and focus on PPP, nonprofit management will not alienate their leaders, employees, donors, or political patrons, as they might if they adopted business practices without modifications. Many nonprofit managers have learned to make these corrections by learning the hard way, making mistakes and then correcting them. Table 6.1 provides a summary of translations from business practices to their analogs in the nonprofits.

The case studies in the book illustrate the difficult-to-understand problems of managing nonprofits. The NMM model is one way to address these problems in a preemptive fashion. We expect that adopting these management tools will bring business-like efficiencies and effectiveness, along with greater accountability, to nonprofits. The suggested

Table 6.1. Translating Business Principles for Nonprofits

Business practices	In a for-profit organization	In a nonprofit organization
Mission	What do you do? Often defined in terms of products and services offered or markets served. What distinguishes a firm from its competition?	What is your cause? What need do you fulfill? Why do you, and not someone else, do this?
Vision	Where do you want your business to be in three or five years? Often defined as specific goals in terms of revenue, profit or customer reach targets, such as being a $5 million company or 30K customers. How do you get there?	How do you want to change the world? What changes can you achieve in three or five years? What would you need to do to get there?
Business model	How does the company make money? For reinvestment and/or as return for its investors? Usually identified as sources of revenue/profit, and quantified performance metrics such as market share or eyeballs to the website.	How do you know that you are being effective? Numbers of people/cases served, instances of problem alleviated, etc. How will you raise the resources to sustain this work? What do the donors care about? How do you deliver on that? How do you prioritize where to focus? Is that criteria consistent with your mission/cause? Is that the most efficient way to achieve the world you are aspiring to create?
Customers	Who will buy your product/service? How do the customers make the purchase decision? What is the customers' willingness to pay? Is the market segmented, and if so how? How is the demand–supply balance?	Who benefits from your service? How do they gain access to your service? Is there adequate need? Do you serve different kinds of clients with differing needs? Do potential clients recognize that they need the offered services?
Investors	Sources of revenue/profit to fund the business, return on equity, long- and short-term loans, venture capitalists or angel investors, etc.	Donors—individual or institutional Foundations—private, charitable, member funded, etc. Government Nongovernment agencies and organizations, including international agencies like the UN or WHO, etc. Collaborations with business organizations
People	Hiring criteria, job descriptions, incentives, training, etc.	All these plus compatibility of values and nonmonetary incentives to engage volunteers, donors, community, and political powers in the organizational processes.
Operations	Physical plant and outlets, processes, legal compliance, supply chains, value chain, input and output logistics, etc.	Locations, access, community ownership, political sensitivity, legal compliance, etc.

modifications to business practices are consistent with the different context in which nonprofit leaders have to manage and achieve their goals.

In conclusion, when making strategy for a nonprofit organization, it is better to frame it in terms of purpose-process-people than the strategy-structure-systems approach. The tools are similar but with some critical and subtle differences. The nonprofit organizations benefit from having clearly articulated mission, vision, and value statements, just like a business enterprise, but instead of having these defined in terms of performance metrics that are profit or growth related, the performance metrics in the nonprofit organization need to be related to social, economic, or environmental impact. The nonfinancial goals of nonprofit organizations are better accomplished with processes that engage people. These process-oriented coordination approaches, with room for individual and contextual variability, allow for followers to be active, creative, and involved with a great deal of personal commitment. The leaders in nonprofit organizations need to rely on their listening skills in order to engage their various stakeholders and build consensus between disparate interests that have some stake in accomplishment of the organizational goals. The leader's role is one of generating connection between individual values and the organizational mission, and thus energizing the followers to participate toward realizing shared goals.

The lessons in this book are consistent with the existing trend of adopting business practices for improved management of nonprofits. The goal has been to unpack the underlying assumptions for these recommendations. We have proposed a set of modifications to business practices that better fit nonprofit organizations. We believe that the basic differences between the two kinds of organizations are a good reason for the need for these. Nonprofits will benefit from moving away from strategy-sturcture-systems toward purpose-process-people.

Case Study Index

THEME: Purpose

THEME: Process

THEME: People

Notes

Chapter 1

1. Ghoshal S., & Bartlett C, (1999).

Chapter 2

1. United Nations State of the World's Children Report (2007).
2. Alanna Young.
3. Salamon (2012), pp. 17–21.
4. John Gardner, quoted *in America's Nonprofit Sector: A Primer*, 3rd Edition (ibid), p. xv.
5. Salamon (2012), pp. 21–24.
6. Heifetz et al. (2009), p. 53.
7. Bridgeland et al. (2009).
8. Bridgeland et al. (2009), p. 3.
9. "More full-time workers volunteer with nonprofits," Sacramento Bee (sacbee.com), February 29, 2012.
10. Ibid, p. 29.
11. Bridgeland et al. (2009), p. 6.
12. "Nonprofit Finance Fund 2012 State of the Sector Survey", p. 1.
13. McClean, C. and Brouwer, C. "The Effect of the Economy on the Nonprofit Sector: A June 2010 Survey," Guidestar, p. 6.
14. Silverthorne (2011, May 12).
15. Illustration concept developed by the authors, and rendered by Tom Benthin.
16. Silverman and Taliento (2006, Summer), p. 41.
17. Wallace N. (2011, April 21).

Chapter 3

1. Phills Jr., J. (2005), p. 21.
2. Bell, Masaoka, and Zimmerman (2010).

Chapter 4

1. Silverman and Taliento (2006, Summer), p. 39.

2. Collins (2005), pp. 9–13.
3. Illustration concept developed by the authors, and rendered by Tom Benthin.
4. Branagh, Kenneth, interviewed by Johnson, Joshua. (2012, April 27) KQED's Forum, Retrieved from http://www.kqed.org/a/forum/R201204271000

Chapter 5

1. Illustration concept by the authors, and rendered by Tom Benthin.

References

Bell, J., Masaoka, J., and Zimmerman, S. (2010). Nonprofit Sustainability. San Francisco: Jossey-Bass.

Bridgeland, J., McNaught, M., Reed, B., & Dunkelman, M., (2009, March). The Quiet Crisis. Michigan: W.K. Kellogg Foundation.

Collins, J. (2005). Good to Great and the Social Sectors: Sectors: A Monograph... to Accompany Good to Great. Denver, CO: Jim Collins (pp. 9–13).

Ghoshal, S., & Bartlett, C. (1999). The Individualized Corporation. New York: HarperCollins.

Glaser, B. G., & Strauss A. L. (1967). The Discovery of Grounded Theory. Chicago, IL: Aldine.

Heifetz, R., Grashow, A., & Linsky, M. (2009). The Practice of Adaptive Leadership: Tools and Tactics for Changing Your Organization and the World. Boston, MA: Harvard Business Press.

Mancuso, A. (2009). How to Form a Nonprofit Corporation in California. Berkeley, CA: Nolo Press.

McCambridge, R and Salamon, L. (March 20, 2003). Nonprofit Quarterly (p. 3).

Philanthropists Start Requiring Management Courses to Keep Nonprofits Productive. *New York Times*, 7/29/11.

Phills Jr., J. (2005). Integrating Mission and Strategy for Nonprofit Organizations. New York: Oxford University Press (p. 21).

Salamon, Lester M. (2012). America's Nonprofit Sector: A Primer. New York: Foundation Center.

Silverman, L., & Taliento, L. (2006, Summer). What Business Execs Don't Know—but Should—About Nonprofits. *Stanford Social Innovation Review 4*, 37–43.

Silverthorne, S. (2011, May 12). The Difficult Transition from For-profit to Non-profit Boards, HBS Working Knowledge series summarizing research by authors Marc J. Epstein of Rice University and F. Warren McFarlan of Harvard Business School in their article Joining a Non-profit Board: What You Need to Know.

Wallace, N. (2011, April 21). A New Breed of Philanthropists Looks to Use Business and Investing to Solve Social Ills. *Chronicle of Philanthropy*.

Additional Resources

A Related Reading List

Nonprofit Sustainability, by Jeanne Bell, Jan Masaoka, and Steve Zimmerman.

Forces for Good: The Six Practices of High-Impact Nonprofits, by Leslie Crutchfield and Heather McLeod Grant.

Managing the Nonprofit Organization, by Peter F. Drucker.

America's Nonprofit Sector: A Primer, by Lester M. Salamon.

The Collaboration Challenge, by James E. Austin.

IRS Publication 557 (Tax-Exempt Status for Your Organization) is a source for legal guidance on these matters.

Nonprofit Management 101: A Complete and Practical Guide for Leaders and Professionals, edited by Darian Rodriguez Heyman.

Integrating Mission and Strategy for Nonprofit Organizations, by James A. Phills, Jr.

Strategic Planning for Non-profit Organizations, by Michael Allison and Jude Kaye.

Strategy for What Purpose by Vijay Sathe in *The Drucker Difference: What the World's Greatest Management Thinker Means to Today's Business Leaders*, edited by Craig L. Pearce, Joseph A. Maciariello Maciareiello, and Hideki Yamawaki.

Embedded Sustainability: The Next Big Competitive Advantage by Chris Laszlo and Nadya Zhexembayeva.

Index

CPSIA information can be obtained at www.ICGtesting.com
Printed in the USA
BVOW030427070613

322666BV00008B/87/P

9 781606 493854